**POCK**

✓ KU-297-842

BARCELONA

Peace and Quiet section by Paul Sterry

© The Automobile Association 1996, 2000.

First published 1992 as *Essential Barcelona*
Revised second edition Jan 1996
Reprinted Apr 1996
Reprinted Sep and Feb 1997
Reprinted Jan and Jun 1998
Reprinted as *Pocket Guide Barcelona* 2000

Maps © The Automobile Association 1996, 2000.

Published by AA Publishing, a trading name of Automobile Association Developments Limited, whose registered office is Norfolk House, Priestley Road, Basingstoke, Hampshire, RG24 9NY.
Registered number 1878835.

Distributed in the United Kingdom by AA Publishing, Norfolk House, Priestley Road, Basingstoke, Hampshire, RG24 9NY.

A CIP catalogue record for this book is available from the British Library.

ISBN 0 7495 2464 2

The Automobile Association retains the copyright in the original edition © 1992 and in all subsequent editions, reprints and amendments.

All rights reserved. No part of this publication may be reproduced, stored in a retrieval system, or transmitted in any form or by any means – electronic, photocopying, recording or otherwise – unless the written permission of the publishers has been obtained beforehand. This book may not be sold, resold, hired out or otherwise disposed of by way of trade in any form of binding or cover other than that in which it is published, without the prior consent of the publisher.
The contents of this publication are believed correct at the time of printing. Nevertheless, the publishers cannot be held responsible for any errors or omissions or for changes in the details given in this guide or for the consequences of any reliance on the information provided by the same. Assessments of attractions, hotels, restaurants and so forth are based upon the author's own experience and, therefore, descriptions given in this guide necessarily contain an element of subjective opinion which may not reflect the publisher's opinion or dictate a reader's own experience on another occasion.

Colour separation: BTB Colour Reproduction Ltd., Whitchurch, Hampshire.

Printed and bound in Italy by Printer Trento srl

Front cover picture: *Sagrada Família* (AA Photo Library – P Wilson)

Contents

Country Distinguishing Signs

On some maps, international distinguishing signs indicate the location of countries around Spain. Thus:

ⒶⓃⒹ = Andorra

Ⓕ = France

This book employs a simple rating system to help choose which places to visit:

✓ 'top ten'

◆◆◆ do not miss
◆◆ see if you can
◆ worth seeing if you have time

INTRODUCTION

Barcelona is a must for the traveller in the
1990s. It is an ancient city, now going through a
frenetic metamorphosis to be in the vanguard
of urban communities in the 21st century. It is
celebrating its past by renovating its old
buildings, and, always innovative, it is
introducing new architecture and extending the
cultural participation of its people.
The amount of things to see and do in Barcelona
is unusually generous for a city of its size. There
is an immensely rich architectural legacy within
its evocative medieval Gothic core. The same is
true in the rest of the city, wherever Modernist
architects raised buildings – challenging when
new (late 19th to early 20th century) and
delightful to see today. Some 40 museums and
lots of art galleries satisfy different interests,
and numerous cultural foundations are very
active in the arts, as are the public authorities.
The city has a strong tradition in music and
theatre, and attracts the world's top performers.
Add to that a mild climate, a varied and
interesting cuisine, fine local wines and plenty
of quality things to buy, including arts and
crafts, antiques, high fashion and other
designer items, and you get an idea of
Barcelona. This is a city of great style – evident
in shops, restaurants, bars, discos and on the
street – and the nightlife is intoxicating.
Most of metropolitan Barcelona's four million
inhabitants celebrated the announcement in

Montjuïc with its commanding view of the city has in the past allowed rulers to command the city's obedience

October 1986 that the city's fourth attempt to attract the summer Olympic Games had been successful. The XXV Olympiad in 1992 was the justification for raising public and private funds to renovate the city, get rid of some severe urban problems and to build for the future. Under the direction of its charismatic mayor, Pasqual Maragall, the city is looking past the Olympics themselves for a continuing programme of change, to shape the city for the year 2000 and beyond.

On two previous occasions Barcelona had used important events to regain confidence, improve and embellish itself and to attract world attention. The Universal Exhibitions of both 1888 and 1929 left legacies of grand buildings – but not much more, because the planning did not go beyond their closing dates. This time, the thinking has been more radical. The renovation inspired by the Olympics has given the city a new face in many places, a better road system, enhanced sports and entertainment facilities, and, it is hoped, a new sense of integration for its less advantaged inhabitants, many of whose origins are elsewhere in Spain.

INTRODUCTION

All this is good news for visitors, although most will still find Barcelona bewitching for the old, intangible reasons. Barcelona somehow casts a spell, and repeated visits do nothing to lessen it – in fact the charm has increased since the mid-1980s, with Barcelona blossoming to become the Mediterranean's most scintillating centre of creativity. The other side to the city's extraordinary character is a tendency to introspection and self-satisfaction among its inhabitants. Outsiders are very rarely made to feel like insiders, and some Barcelonans give the impression of thinking that Barcelona is the centre of the universe. The reality is impressive enough however. The city is the buzzing nerve centre of a dynamic and industrious region – Barcelona is the capital of Catalunya, traditionally Spain's most culturally progressive and economically advanced region, and still at the forefront today. Reason enough, perhaps, for the Barcelonan's special sense of pride.

Tibidabo looks over the city and its suburbs to the Mediterranean

BACKGROUND

To understand Barcelona, you have to know
about Catalunya (otherwise known as Cataluña
or Catalonia). Catalunya, in the northeast of
Spain, is one of its 17 semi-autonomous regions
– still part of the Spanish state, but with a good
deal of independence. The regions have been
created in the progress to democracy within a
federal system since the death of the dictator
General Franco in 1975. Catalunya has around
15 per cent of Spain's population of 39 million
and six per cent of Spain's territory, but as the
country's most economically advanced region,
it produces around 20 per cent of Spain's gross
domestic product. Within its four provinces it
offers wide physical variety: high Pyrenean
peaks and lush valleys in Lleida and Girona
provinces; Lleida's bare and rugged
landscapes; one of the world's best known
holiday areas, the pine-backed coastline of the
Costa Brava (Girona province); the acclaimed
vineyards of Penedés and the serrated heights
of Montserrat mountain within Barcelona
province; and the wetlands of the Ebro Delta in
Tarragona province. The city of Barcelona, now
a sprawling metropolitan area of over four
million people, is Catalunya's capital. Just under
two million live within Barcelona's municipal
area itself. It is there that the Catalan parliament
has its seat and from where the *Generalitat*, the
executive branch, directs the region's affairs
under a statute from the central government in
Madrid, which many Catalans believe is still too
restrictive of their freedoms. The municipal
area of Barcelona is run by the *Ajuntament*. In
recent years, the Generalitat has been
controlled by a right of centre party with
nationalist aspirations, and the Ajuntament has
been run by the Catalan socialist party, with
different views about what is best for the city,
especially in the past over matters related to the
Olympic Games. No visitor to Barcelona can for
long remain unaware of two personalities: the
president of the Generalitat, and the *alcalde*
(mayor) of Barcelona. The palaces which are
their seats of power face each other across
Plaça de Sant Jaume, where once there was a
Roman market place and, most likely, a good

Not seeing eye to eye: the palace of the Ajuntament (top) and Generalitat (bottom) face one another

deal of bartering went on, then as now. A very small nationalist movement calls for the complete independence of Catalunya from Spain. The main nationalist aspiration is for greater autonomy within the Spanish state. Catalans complain that they are more industrious than other Spaniards and that they fill coffers which Madrid empties wastefully in other parts of the country. They want greater freedom in foreign relations and, to the annoyance of Madrid, the president of the Generalitat makes many official visits abroad. He has also initiated an organisation for

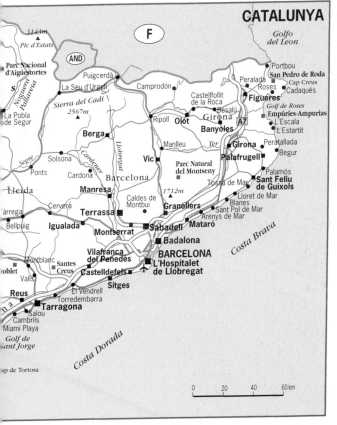

CATALUNYA

economic and political co-operation with other regions in Europe and North America. Catalans believe that, because of a different historical experience, they have learned other, better ways of doing things which it will be to their advantage to apply in running the affairs of their region. They also claim to have been a nation centuries before there was a united Spain: the Catalans are a people with a distinct language and culture, found not only in the present-day region of Catalunya, but also in the regions of Valencia and the Balearic Islands, as well as in Andorra and southern France.

BACKGROUND

The Catalan language developed from a version of Latin spoken in the northern regions of present-day Catalunya, and was widely spoken by the 9th century. Its great flowering as a written language happened in the 15th century. From the next century onwards it was rather obscured under the pressure of Castilian, which became the standard Spanish of today. In the early 1800s, however, during what is known as the *renaixença* or Catalan renaissance, there was a revival of interest in all things Catalan. The language flourished again over the following century, which culminated in 1932 with the publishing of the *Diccionari General*, the standard dictionary for the Catalan language. During the early years of Franco's rule it was forbidden to speak Catalan in public, but the language never died out. Today Catalan is an offical language in Catalunya, ranking equally with Castilian Spanish. Catalan has also been officially recognised by the European Parliament, and was designated well beforehand as an official language of the XXV Olympiad. Its use is widespread in the media, business, cultural institutions and places of education.

Franco also threatened the Catalan language and culture in a more insidious way. From the 1950s he encouraged massive immigration to Catalunya from poorer regions of Spain such as Andalucia and Murcia, with the aim of watering down Catalan culture. Almost a million migrants arrived, mostly to work in and around Barcelona, where they lived in depressing, low-cost housing. Some did not find work, and neither have their children. Many have not integrated into Catalan society and it is unlikely that they will do so. It is widely said that the people from southern Spain are lazy, though nobody who has seen a construction worker or farmer working hard for very long hours in the hot sun can accept that proposition. However, they may be more willing to put off a job until tomorrow (*mañana*) whereas Catalans have a stricter work discipline and are generally eager to get on with a productive, well-rewarded career, whether it be in business or the arts. Catalans consider themselves to have the quality of *seny*, sound judgement, which makes them different from other Spaniards. Traditionally they have been more open to foreign influences and new trends than their compatriots, which has been to their advantage economically and culturally. This could be because of where they are on the European map, though some claim it is because of a cool and calculating temperament, more mid-European than Mediterranean. Elsewhere in Spain, it has been members of the landed aristocracy who have dominated society and been patrons of the arts. In Barcelona, it has been the mercantile class that has had most influence. The business community built fine mansions and sponsored the arts in the Middle Ages, and continues to do so. Cultural organisations founded by banks (*caixas*) are prominent, and business firms are paying for the restoration of long-neglected buildings, monuments and fountains around the city. Surprisingly in a city where business attitudes and influence are so strong, there is also an attitude that 'anything goes', and you have freedom to be what you like.

Creatively and morally Barcelona is a very open city – too much so for some visitors when they see what is sometimes presented as creative talent, or notice the hundreds of sex advertisements in the columns of quality

Fairytale Spain in the Poble Espanyol

BACKGROUND

Miró, Miró on the wall – and on the floor in the Fundació Miró

newspapers. There is no doubt about the benefits to real creativity, however.

Artists working in Barcelona have gained great international acclaim. Among big names are Picasso, Miró, Rusinyol and Tàpies, principally painters; the architects include Gaudí and Sert; and among the musicians are Pau Casals, Montserrat Caballé and Josep Carreras. A few of the new names to be aware of are Miquel Barceló and Thomas Gomez, both painters; the sculptor Susana Solana; architects Bofill, Bohigas, Mackay, Martorell and Puig Domènech; designers Mariscal and Arribas; and the fashion designers Lola Barceló and José Tomas.

Visiting Barcelona

Guidebooks usually say the local people are friendly and welcoming. About Barcelonans it is more accurate to say they are correctly courteous to all visitors and that they are very welcoming to business people and people of artistic talent. Mr and Mrs Ordinary on a medium-cost holiday can expect fewer smiles than the industrialists, bankers and importers on business trips; and a city so much in the vanguard of contemporary culture gives a great welcome to any stars in the international arts galaxy. It also provides a friendly and encouraging environment for creative people who are talented but still unknown.

Barcelona has been best known as a city of trade and industry. Founded as a Roman trading and administrative post, it reached its zenith as leader among the Mediterranean's medieval port cities. In the 18th century, after centuries of obscurity, its textile industry again brought wealth and influence, and today it leads once more among port cities of the Mediterranean. It is a major industrial city and has growing significance as a financial centre. Curiously, neither the private nor public sectors have extensively exploited the tourism potential of Barcelona. It is as if the Barcelonans, who control Catalunya's purse strings, have thought that high-volume tourism was something which should only happen in the summer along Catalunya's coast – the Costa Brava, Costa Maresme and Costa Dorada. During weekdays it is difficult to find hotel accommodation in the city, as rooms are occupied by visitors to the city's many trade fairs and conferences. New hotels are being built, but too few to relieve the problem significantly. Tourist authorities have, by necessity, promoted the city as a weekend break destination. It is ideal for that, if you just want a taste, but Barcelona demands much more time to discover.

A solution to the accommodation problem is to stay during weekdays at one of the coastal resorts, from Blanes to Tarragona, which have a regular rail connection to Barcelona, and to make daily excursions to the city. Then stay in the city over the weekend and make the most of its exuberant nightlife.

Most tourists come in high summer when it is hot and humid. In spring and autumn the weather is more agreeable however, and people are not skulking in the shade but enjoying the streets, parks and outdoor cafés. Outdoor Barcelona can also be enjoyed on the many clear, but sometimes very crisp, winter days. The weather makes Barcelona an all-year destination, and the calendar of cultural events is full throughout the year.

Visitors must bear in mind, however, that Spain generally is no longer the country for low-cost holidays, and in Barcelona prices have risen well above the national average.

Barcelona has two problems common to most large cities. Tourists complain most about the city's pollution and street crime. A thick layer of polluted air often hangs, unmoving, above the city, and the streets are blocked with traffic four times a day as private cars, buses, taxis and goods vehicles noisily do battle for space. Civil action groups are trying to encourage the greater use of public transport while new roads are being built and faster traffic flow schemes introduced. The wider use of lead-free petrol and better emission controls on vehicles and factories will help but it is also likely that with increasing affluence there will be more and more cars coming on to Barcelona's roads. Then there are parts of the city, like either side of La Rambla towards the port, which visitors should quite simply avoid for their personal safety; other danger areas are some parts of metro and bus lines. Much of the street crime is committed to sustain a personal drug dependence, and there are drug rehabilitation schemes to combat the problem. The authorities are also smartening some of the most run down areas in the inner city where crime breeds, fed by deprivation. Visitors can play their part by taking the precautions sensible in any city.

The Making of Barcelona

Barcelona's present shape and appearance have evolved over many centuries. In prehistoric times, Iberian people lived in the hinterland of present-day Barcelona, and the Laietani tribe had a settlement in close proximity. Phoenician and Greek traders are known to have visited these shores and the Carthaginians set up an encampment named Barcino after the general, Hamilcar Barca. Roman Barcelona dates from the 2nd century BC and was centred on the low mound of Mont Taber, which is almost at the heart of the Barri Gòtic. It grew to be a trading and administrative town of some 30 acres (12 hectares) under the jurisdiction of the very much larger town of Tarraco (Tarragona). Parts remain of the town wall which dates from the late 3rd century, and excavations under the Plaça del Rei and the Museu d'Història de la Ciutat have revealed

ruins of the Roman town. They also show traces of the sojourn of the Visigoths, who made Barcelona their capital in the Iberian peninsula for a brief period in the 6th century.
There is no evidence that the Moors and Franks, who in turn controlled the town over the next centuries, prized it highly or expanded it. In the 870s counties of the Franks south of the Pyrenees became united under Count Wilfred the Hairy (878–97) and thereby the House of the Counts of Barcelona was founded. With the expansion of the court and religious institutions Barcelona began to experience real growth. By the 12th century, trade within the Mediterranean was already extensive and this grew faster during the reign of Ramon Berenguer IV (1131–62). Through the marriage of this count, Catalunya and the neighbouring kingdom of Aragón joined in a federation under a single crown but with each keeping its laws, language and customs. The federation took Mallorca, Ibiza and Valencia from the Moors during the reign of Jaume I, The Conqueror (1213–76). Trade had another big boost and in Barcelona there was much building, including new town walls around an area some 10 times bigger than that enclosed by the previous walls. Mercenary admirals Roger de Lluria and Roger de Flor, who became great folk heroes, helped the count-kings of Barcelona and Aragón acquire Sicily, Athens, Corsica and

Roman foundations on display in the Museu d'Historia de la Ciutat

Sardinia by 1324, when Barcelona was at the zenith of its power. Under Jaume II (1276–1327) more big building projects, including the great Gothic cathedral, were started. Pere IV (1336–87) was also a keen builder, one of whose projects was the beautiful Saló del Tinell. In Catalunya the power of the count-king came under the scrutiny of the Corts, a parliament of three chambers made up of the nobility, clergy and mercantile class. The aristocracy and rich merchants were also active builders, commissioning their fine houses within what is today called the Barri Gòtic, and along streets like Carrer Montcada. All this went on while the Black Death, which broke out in 1348, and other plagues were decimating the population. In 1359, the Corts created the Generalitat, an executive of 24 members, to manage the country's budget. By the end of the 14th century, the Barri Gòtic, as we see it now, had largely taken its final shape, and Barcelona had been endowed with one of the world's most beautiful and evocative city districts. But the city had by then also entered a period of socio-political difficulties and eventual economic decline.

The line of the House of Barcelona ended when Martin I died without an heir in 1410, and Catalunya became a partner in the crown of the burgeoning central kingdom of Castile. It retained its ancient rights, *constitucions*, by which the monarch's powers were limited in Catalunya. The Catalan civil war between 1462

The 19th century saw the city grow at breakneck speed

and 1473 wrecked the economy and, although there was some recovery, Catalunya was of less interest to Castilian rulers looking west towards the Americas after 1492. (Barcelona was specifically excluded from trade with the Americas.) During the War of the Spanish Succession (1700–14), Catalunya, and especially Barcelona, opposed the Bourbon claimant, Felipe V, but he was eventually recognised as king and punished the Catalans by revoking their *constitucions*. Although there was much bitterness, Barcelona's business community initiated a slow recovery. Trade with the Americas was again permitted, textile industrialisation began and there was a big growth in population. The Napoleonic Wars (early 1800s) halted the forward movement, and poverty and disease helped fuel the social unrest which sparked sporadic outbursts of mass violence through the 19th century. The Barcelona business community, ever eager to get on with profit making, saw to it that there was economic progress in spite of the local unrest and Spain's political chaos during this time. Increasing profitability from mechanisation of the textile industry was the main plank for the growing wealth of this group. It supported the *renaixença*, an awakening of interest and pride in all things Catalan from poetry to architecture.

By the mid-19th century, the very rapidly growing population made extension of the city essential, and a competition was arranged to find the best urban plan. Ildefons Cerdà won the competition of 1859 with his very formalised, modern scheme for the *Eixample* ('Extension' in Catalan), and work began 10 years later. Meanwhile civic and business confidence was booming, and Barcelona decided to show itself off to the world. The Universal Exhibition of 1888 attracted over two million visitors to its site based around the Parc de la Ciutadella. Montjuïc hill was the main site for Barcelona's next Universal Exhibition in 1929. In the intervening 41 years the city had seen a doubling of the population, unplanned growth, strikes, anarchy and terrorism of which the most remembered outbreak is the *Setmana Tràgica* (Tragic Week) of 1909, when some 70 religious buildings were destroyed. There had also been the coming and going of the *Modernista* (Modernist) architects and craftspeople. They created for the city an architectural heritage which, together with its Gothic inheritance and much of what is being raised today, gives Barcelona a just claim to be among the world's richest cities architecturally.

Modernism

In the latter part of the 19th century artistic trends in several countries developed into what can conveniently be grouped together as Art Nouveau. The trend in Catalunya was called Modernism and it showed important distinctions from the others: it had strong nationalist overtones, and became the fullest expression of the Catalan *renaixença*. It was widely adopted with enthusiasm by the wealthy Barcelonans. The visitor's first encounter with Modernism (and he or she cannot easily escape it) will probably be the façades of the many mansion blocks, mainly in the Eixample, which were designed for the wealthy by architects such as Antoni Gaudí, Domènech i Montaner, Puig i Cadalfach, Josep Vilaseca and others.

Modernism also found expression in the crafts used to decorate the buildings: those of the sculptor, ceramicist, glazier, ironworker, woodworker and cabinet-maker. But it also influenced painting, sculpture, graphic art, literature, bookbinding and even the way people dressed and conducted their lives. In one of those anomalies of Barcelona, a revolutionary artistic trend became almost the philosophy of its most conservative group. There were always some who detested Modernism – for them it was tasteless and excessive – but the general enthusiasm for it lasted until the 1920s (the new trend then was *noucentisme*, a return to classical inspiration which was shared with much of Europe).

The dominant style, inspiration for Modernist architects, was Catalan Gothic, which permitted them to celebrate the architectural achievements of Catalunya's golden age. To this they added more or less what they liked – usually extensive decoration, using varying combinations of crafts. Domènech i Montaner's Palau de la Música Catalana is one of the best examples of the use of mixed decoration. What might at first seem to be the most unacceptable juxtaposition of subjects, styles and materials comes together in a whole of great harmony. The master of Modernism however was Antoni Gaudí. He graduated in 1878 and his earliest architectural work showed the influence of Catalan Gothic. In buildings such as the Casa Vicens and Palau Güell, both completed in 1888, he added elements of the Mudéjar style developed by medieval Moorish craftsmen in Spain. But his principal inspiration for form soon became nature itself – its flowing lines and organic shapes. This posed many technical difficulties for which he found audacious solutions. Gaudí's work is also distinguished by the uniquely creative ornamentation of his buildings. He worked closely with some of the leading craftspeople to furnish the architectural spaces he created with wrought iron, stained glass, sculpture and mosaics as well as

The attraction of Gaudí's work is not just its dramatic scale but also the superb detail, as here in the Parc Güell

furniture itself. The Güells, a family of rich industrialists, were Gaudí's main patrons, giving him many commissions and introductions. A religious zeal which found release in his work on the Sagrada Família cathedral overwhelmed his later years. In 1926 he died in a Barcelona hospital, unrecognised because of his scruffiness. The city's most famous architect had been run over by a tram.

The Extraordinary Works of Gaudí

The unique architectural styles of the Catalan Antonio Gaudí continue to attract much attention. In addition to the Sagrada Família, world famous symbol of Barcelona, the following works of Gaudí can be seen in the city: Casa Batlló; Casa Vicens; Pavellons de la Finca Güell; Colegi de les Teresianes; Casa Calvet; Torre Bellesguard; Palau Güell; Casa Milà (La Pedrera) and Parc Güell.

Infighting between anarchists and socialists undermined the Republican cause

Dark Years

Spain's king, Alfonso XIII, fled the country in 1931 when it was clear from municipal elections that the electorate wanted a republic. Francesc Macià, previously exiled, became president of the Generalitat. Spain declared the Second Republic, but by the end of 1935, 28 governments in Madrid, of varying complexions, had been unable to stabilise the chaos in the nation. The Popular Front, an alliance of the Left, gained power after elections in February 1936, but chaos continued. In July, army factions, so-called Nationalists, led by General Franco, rose against the government. The ensuing Civil War was horrific. The Republican government was based in Barcelona from May 1937 until the city was taken by the Nationalists in January 1939. It was a period of anarchy and faction rivalry but also of heroism and fortitude.

Barcelona shared in Spain's post-war privations but it was the first city to show recovery. Again the business community was demonstrating its *seny* by working to its own advantage within a new order. Although public manifestations of Catalanism were forbidden, clandestine support of their separate language and culture gave Barcelonans the spirit to rise above the dullness of Franco's oppressive centralism. During the dark years it remained more in touch with the outside world, and retained a vitality not found elsewhere in Spain. From the 1950s there was strong economic progress, as well as the massive immigration and ugly, unplanned growth which created many of today's urban problems.

Orientation

The city spreads across a flat area of some 12 square miles (20 sq km) between the Mediterranean on the east and a semicircle of hills running from the southeast to the northwest. It is divided into municipal districts which in turn are divided into *barris*. Montjuïc hill rises to 570 feet (173m) and a vantage point towards its seaward side is a good place from which to get a panorama of the city's principal areas of interest. Montjuïc itself is certainly one of those. Looking northeast along the coast is the old harbour, now part of a grand development which has included extensive remodelling of the original Barceloneta fishing quarters, with new marinas, promenades and the creation of the new Olympic Village residential zone.

Looking inland, directly below Montjuïc is the barri of Poble Sec, and beyond the broad Avinguda del Paral-lel is the district of Ciutat Vella (Old Town) with its barris of Raval, Casc Antic and Sant Pere-Ribera, separated from each other by the northwest to southeast arteries of La Rambla (not to be missed) and Via Laietana respectively. La Rambla (or Las Ramblas) is a series of five streets forming one long avenue through the city. At its foot, Columbus stands atop his tall pedestal pointing in the wrong direction for America, which often confuses visitors. At the core of the Casc Antic (Old Quarter), there is the beautiful, medieval Barri Gòtic. Principal tourist attractions within Sant Pere-Ribera are the Carrer Montcada and Parc de la Ciutadella.

Plaça de Catalunya, communications hub of the city, lies at the upper end of La Rambla. North and west of it stretches the extensive regular pattern of the Eixample district, dissected by three grand avenues: Gran Via de les Corts Catalanes (northeast to southwest); Passeig de Gràcia (northwest to southeast); and Avinguda Diagonal (west to east).

Beyond Avinguda Diagonal and stretching into the lower reaches of the Collserola hills are the residential districts of Horta Guinardo, Gràcia and Sarria Sant Gervasi. The district of Les Corts lies at the southern end of Avinguda Diagonal and includes the barris of Pedralbes and Les Corts.

Tibidabo, 1,740 feet (532m), is the highest point of the Collserola hills. A big attraction is now the impressive development project of the old port, including the Port Vell de Barcelona and Port Olímpic. Suburbs of low-cost housing and industrial zones stretch north and south of the central city. Beyond lie the attractions of the beach resorts of Barcelona province: to the north, the Costa Maresme with resorts like Arenys de Mar and Mataró; to the south, the Costa Dorada with resorts like Castelldefels

*Once a riverbed,
the tree-lined
La Rambla runs
down to the sea*

and Sitges. The airport is seven and a half miles (12km) south of the city and is served by both rail and bus connections.

1992 and Beyond

The year 1992 was earmarked well in advance as one of special significance in Spain, as the 500th anniversary of Cristobal Colom's (Christopher Columbus') first voyage of discovery, the year of EXPO'92 in Sevilla (the biggest-ever Universal Exhibition), Madrid's designation as European City of Culture and the Olympic Games in Barcelona from 25 July to 9 August. The people of Barcelona resigned themselves early on to the disruption and inconvenience of preparation for the Olympics, as a price for enhancement of the city, including solutions to some urgent urban problems.

Indeed this more than proved to be the case. The new developments of the old port area, sports venues, Olympic village, new hotels, reopened shoreline and construction of the 'Rondas,' or ring roads, have changed the face of Barcelona. The Barcelonans are justifiably proud of these achievements, which have brought about the transformation of Barcelona to a city of the future.

The Port Vell development is considered to be one of the most ambitious port remodelling projects in the world. Covering an area of some 136 acres (55 hectares), it constitutes the opening up of the port to the city. At a cost of over 50,000 million pesetas, involving both the public and private sector, it has been a project of great magnitude, comprising three basic areas. The Moll Barcelona is dominated by a new International Trade Centre, due to be completed in 1996, with offices, convention facilities, restaurants and parking. The Moll España has been transformed into a leisure, cultural and commercial centre joined to La Rambla by a new bridge. Special attractions are a vast aquarium and the newly opened Maremàgnum complex of eight cinematographic halls. 'Golondrina' boat trips operate from here around the harbour. Within the Moll Barceloneta are shops, offices, bars and restaurants, in addition to the Museu de Historia de Catalunya. A promenade leads past the Vila Olímpica (Olympic Village). Built on an old disused factory site, this now provides living accommodation overlooking the sea and has evolved as a new district which has become an integral part of the city. Further along is the Port Olímpic, with its attractive yacht harbour, water sports facilities and trendy open-air bars and restaurants. There are plans to extend the promenade well beyond the outskirts of the city, providing a splendid stroll along some three miles (5km) of cleaned-up sandy beaches. The area is much favoured by the local people and weekends usually see plenty of activity

The construction of two ring roads, 'Ronda del Litoral' and 'Ronda de Dalt', major components in the scheme to alleviate Barcelona's traffic congestion problems, has resulted in a 15 to 20 per cent reduction in city traffic, together with a 30 per cent reduction in pollution. Better sports facilities are also offered in the Anella Olímpica (Olympic Ring), which contains the re-styled Olympic Stadium and Sports Complex.

Remodelling of the Estació d'Autobuses Barcelona Nord (Barcelona Nord Coach Station) has for the first time given Barcelona a central bus station for all long-distance services within the peninsula and abroad. The França railway station (Estació de França), for long-

Face to the Sea

'Cara al Mar' (Face to the Sea) is Barcelona's new image, denoting a city which is now open to the sea. The extensive development of the port area provides an important leisure area for the people of Barcelona, who can enjoy the coastal promenades, sandy beaches, yacht marinas and lively open-air bars and restaurants. This has become a very popular area for the local people, especially at weekends when they can enjoy the feeling of taking a short holiday.

distance and international trains, has undergone considerable improvement, with development in the surrounding area for an exhibition hall, hotel and gardens. There have been extensions to metro lines, improvements to stations and the provision of new rolling stock. The redevelopment of the old port includes an international trade centre and a marina, plus commercial, cultural, recreational and sports facilities. It is also another opening of the city to the sea, which is a novelty for Barcelonans. The British architect Norman Foster designed the elegant Torre de Telecommunicaciones, rising to 853 feet (260m) on Tibidabo, to replace the many telecommunications installations which previously defaced the hill.

On the site of old railyards adjoining the Estació del Nord two grand cultural buildings are

The new Olympic Stadium on the crest of Montjuïc can seat some 60,000 spectators

BACKGROUND

There are fine views across the city from the top of the Monument a Colom

rising. The Teatre Nacional has been designed by Ricardo Bofill, with a winter garden vestibule, library, exhibition hall and two auditoria (1,000 and 500 capacities) below its metal and glass roof. The Auditori has been designed by Rafael Moneo around a central patio crowned by a semi-open cupola, to provide a fully integrated centre for the performance, practice and study of music. Barcelona has several important new museums and centres. One such, located in the cultural belt of the old city, parallel to the Rambla, is the Centre de Cultura Contemporánia de Barcelona and adjoining Museu d'Art Contemporani de Barcelona, designed by Richard Meier and due to have opened in 1995. They form part of the redevelopment of the Casa de la Caritat convent into a centre of contemporary culture. In the Pedralbes district is the new Fundació Collección Thyssen-Bornemisza.

Along with all this new building goes the redevelopment of dilapidated areas like the old red light zone of Barri Xines, and the *nou urbanisme* programme of embellishing urban spaces with outstanding design and art. This is a new Barcelona, which looks seawards; a city which has undergone two major transformations: the challenge of the 1992 Olympics and that of the new United Europe, resulting in the creation of new roads systems, hotels, commercial complexes and better services. Some may mourn the passing of a certain colourful sleaziness, but Barcelona is approaching the year 2,000 with all the zest and style that makes it one of Europe's most exciting cities.

WHAT TO SEE

There is a lot to see, and you will have to pace yourself to avoid physical and mental exhaustion. An overload of culture and nightlife is a real danger in this city. Allow time for just strolling and looking at the buildings – Barcelona's architecture is something to be savoured, so this book includes entries on the most interesting city districts as well as places to visit within them. Allow time for shopping and window shopping too. Start your planning by getting a map. The one given free by municipal tourist offices is adequate, but you can buy more comprehensive maps at kiosks or bookshops.

Museums and Cultural Centres

Even if you are not greatly interested in the subject matter of Barcelona's museums, you may want to see many of them because of their buildings. Except for the Museu Etnològic and the Fundació Miró, they are housed in buildings which have been converted for the purpose and are often interesting in their own right. The Museu Picasso may be at the top of your itinerary anyway, but even those who have an aversion to the artist's work should try to see it – the museum occupies two Gothic palaces. Opposite on Carrer Montcada, another fine

Barcelona's dreaming spires

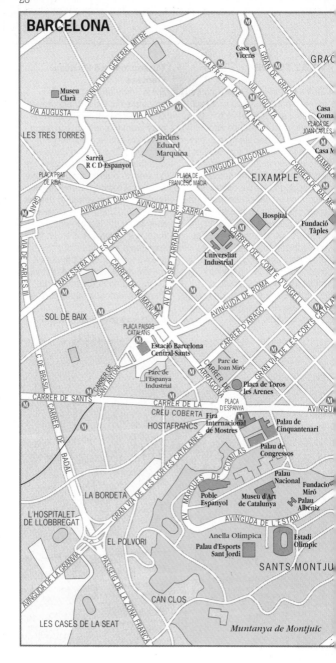

BARCELONA

Casa Vicens

C. GRAN DE GRACIA

GRAC

Museu Clarà

RONDA DEL GENERAL MITRE

CARRER DE

VIA AUGUSTA

VIA AUGUSTA

VIA AUGUSTA

BALMES

Casa Coma

PLAÇA DE JOAN CARLES

LES TRES TORRES

Jardins Eduard Marquina

Casa M

Sarrià R C D Espanyol

AVINGUDA DIAGONAL

CARRER DE BALME

PLAÇA PRAT DE RIBA

PLAÇA DE FRANCESC MACIA

EIXAMPLE

RAMBLA

GRAN

AVINGUDA DIAGONAL

AVINGUDA DE SARRIA

Hospital

Fundació Tàples

VIA DE CARLES III

TRAVESSERA DE LES CORTS

CARRER DE NUMANCIA

AV DE JOSEP TARRADELLAS

Universitat Industrial

CARRER DEL COMTE D'URGELL

AVINGUDA DE ROMA

CARRER DE LES CORTS CATALA

SOL DE BAIX

PLAÇA PAISOS CATALANS

AVINGUDA D'ARAGO

Estació Barcelona Central-Sants

CARRER DE TARRAGONA

Parc de Joan Miró

GRAN VIA DE LES CORTS

C. DE BRASIL

CARRER DE SANT ANTONI

Parc de l'Espanya Industrial

Plaça de Toros les Arenes

CARRER DE SANTS

CARRER DE LA CREU COBERTA

PLAÇA D'ESPANYA

AVINGU

CARRER DE BADAL

Fira Internacional de Mostres

Palau de Cinquantenari

HOSTAFRANCS

Palau de Congressos

AV. MARQUES DE COMILAS

Palau Nacional

Fundacio Miró

LA BORDETA

GRAN VIA DE LES CORTES CATALANES

Poble Espanyol

Museu d'Art de Catalunya

Palau Albeniz

L'HOSPITALET DE LLOBBREGAT

AVINGUDA DE L'ESTADI

EL POLVORI

Anella Olímpica

Estadi Olímpic

AVINGUDA DE LA GRANJA

Palau d'Esports Sant Jordi

SANTS-MONTJU

PASSEIG DE LA ZONA FRANCA

CAN CLOS

LES CASES DE LA SEAT

Muntanya de Montjuïc

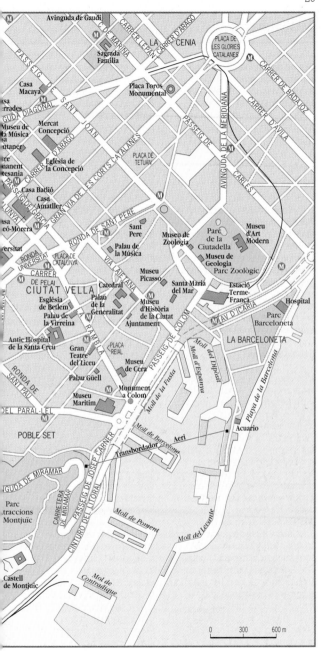

Gothic palace houses the Museu Tèxtil i de la Indumentària – worth a visit even if you have little interest in textiles and clothing. You need not be very keen on things maritime to appreciate the Gothic grandeur of the Museu Marítim; by way of contrast, a Modernist mansion, the Casa Quadras, is home to the Museu de la Música. The same goes for cultural centres: that of the Caixa de Pensions in Passeig Sant Joan is Casa Macaya, another building by the Modernist Puig i Cadalfach. Most museums are closed on Mondays and public holidays. Entrance fees vary but none are very high. The main museums are described here, but there are many others, on subjects from geology to shoemaking.

Urban Spaces

Visitors to Barcelona have something new to appreciate around the city: a bold attempt to make contemporary art part of the scenery. This is of greater significance in Barcelona than in most cities: within its *nou urbanisme* scheme, Barcelona is both creating urban spaces (*espais urbans*), or remodelling existing ones, which are being endowed with sculptures and design by leading contemporary artists. *Nou urbanisme* includes strict control on the quality of design and construction of new buildings. The Australian-born writer on architecture, Robert Hughes, an admirer of Barcelona, has described it as 'the most ambitious project of its kind undertaken by the Town Hall of any city in the 20th century', and

in his recent memoirs, the architect Ricardo Bofill has written, 'We architects of Barcelona have learned anew how to make a city.'

A selection of urban spaces and architectural features is included in the entries which follow. (*Parc* means park; *plaça* means square or plaza.) If time is very short and you want to get some idea of the city's *nou urbanisme*, three very different examples of what is being done can be seen in the vicinity of Estaciò Sants: Plaça Països Catalans, Parc de l'Espanya Industrial and Parc de Joan Miró. But keep aware as you move around the city, and everywhere you will find evidence of this weaving of art into Barcelona's fabric.

Bus Turístic (Bus 100)

From mid-June to mid-October, between 09.00 and 19.30 hours the Bus Turístic (Bus 100) makes a circuit with 15 stops convenient for the main places of interest. The ticket is purchased on board and there are two types: one-day or two-day. Service starts and ends at Plaça de Catalunya. The ticket allows unrestricted use and unlimited travel on five means of transport: Bus 100, Telefèric de Montjuïc, Funicular de Montjuïc, Tramvia Blau and Funicular del Tibidabo. More information and a route map can be obtained from tourist offices and TMB kiosks such as the one below Plaça de Catalunya. In the descriptions of places which follow, the stop number of Bus 100 is given in brackets. Remember it runs only for a limited period of the year.

◆◆◆
ANELLA OLÍMPICA
Montjuïc

The Olympic Ring spreads over the western crest of Montjuïc hill. The stadium built for the Universal Exhibition of 1929, with the Olympics of 1936 in mind, was gutted except for the façade, and the new **Estadi Olímpic** was designed by architects Gregotti, Milà, Correa, Buxadè and Margarit. Gargallo's sculpture of the chariot racer, *Els Aurugues*, and the monumental marathon entrance gate have been retained. The old stadium site required excavating 36 feet (11m) to increase the seating capacity to 60,000.

Japanese architect Arata Isozaki coupled traditional architectural principles with modern technology and materials in his design of the **Palau d'Esports Sant Jordi**. For instance, the huge cupola is supported like that of Florence cathedral and requires no interior pillars, which would restrict views in the arena. It can seat 17,000 spectators and has a six-lane athletics track with a perimeter of 656 feet (200 metres). The cupola allows in daylight to save on lighting costs and also has acoustic panels, because the Palau Sant Jordi is also a venue for concerts. It was the single most impressive and expensive building raised for the Olympic Games.

Sculptures in the adjoining plaça are by Aiko Miyawaku. The other sports complex within the Anella Olímpica, the **Complex Esportiu Bernat Picornell**, has two pools used for swimming, waterpolo and synchronised swimming. There is a new baseball field with stands for 1,000 spectators.

Ricardo Bofill had a Greco-Roman inspiration for his design of the Generalitat's **Institut Nacional de Educació Fisica** (INEF). This sports university

Olympic Stadium – great teamwork

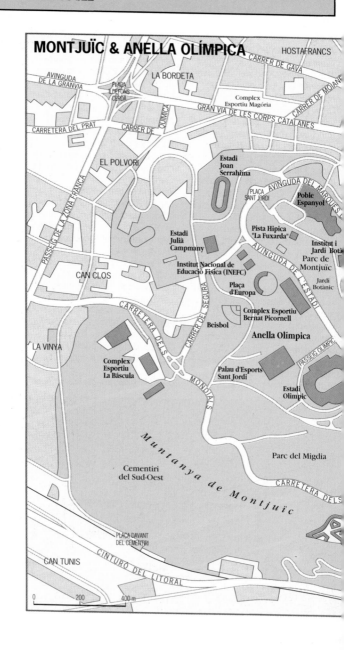

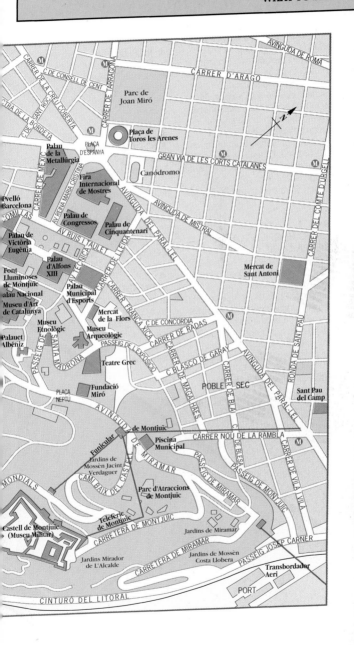

has facilities for 1,000 students and 100 teachers and is arranged around two cloisters. Joining them is a vestibule and a hall for exhibitions and performances with a capacity of 2,000. The various installations are linked with three plaças, united by stairs and a huge cascade of water, built upon one of Europe's biggest water tanks. The *depósito* holds 78,000 cubic yards (60,000 cu m).
Buses: 61 from Plaça d'Espanya; 100 (stop 11).

◆◆
ANTIC HOSPITAL DE LA SANTA CREU
between Carrer de l'Hospital and Carrer del Carme
This institution was first established in the 11th century as a hospice for ailing pilgrims. It makes a handsome assembly of Gothic buildings, now used by Catalan educational and cultural organisations. You can

The exhibitionist Arc del Triomf

visit its peaceful courtyards and view the buildings from the outside. The chapel is used for exhibitions (details from tourist offices and the local press).
Metro: Liceu. *Bus*: 100 (stops 1 and 13).

◆
ARC DEL TRIOMF
Passeig de Lluis Companys
The arch symbolises the 1888 Universal Exhibition, to which it was the main entrance. With sponsorship from the department store chain El Corte Inglés, it has been restored to its former glory.
Metro: Arc del Triomf.

◆
AVINGUDA DE GAUDÍ
Avinguda de Gaudí is a broad avenue joining two of the city's architectural sights: Gaudí's Sagrada Família and Domènech i Montaner's lesser-known Hospital de la Santa Creu i Sant Pau. As part of the *nou urbanisme* programme, the

avenue has been redesigned by M Quintana to have a central walkway decorated with antique streetlamps and sculptures by Apel·les Fenosa.

BARRI GÒTIC
(see **CIUTAT VELLA DISTRICT** pages 39–40)

◆
CAROUSEL DE LA GUARDA URBANA
La Fuxarda Pista Hípica, Parc de Montjuïc
The Carousel is a 40-minute display of horsemanship by the mounted troop of the municipal police. Thursdays, June to September, starting at 22.00hrs. *Metro*: Plaça d'Espanya.

◆◆◆
CASA AMATLLER
Passeig de Gràcia 41
The architect Puig i Cadafalch had Nordic Gothic inspiration when he began work on this apartment block in 1898. Note the finish, bold for its time, and the elegance of the ceramic tiling. With Gaudí's Casa Batlló and Domènech i Montaner's Casa Lleó-Morera, it makes up the so-called Manzana de Discordia, or Block of Discord. *Open*: Tuesday to Saturday 10.00–14.00hrs; may be open some evenings. *Metro*: Passeig de Gràcia. *Bus*: 100 (stop 2).

◆◆◆
CASA BATLLÓ
Passeig de Gràcia 43
Both inside and outside, Gaudí showed his brilliance with natural forms when he remodelled this apartment block between 1904 and 1906. It has a

wealth of undulating forms, different motifs, and bright and subtle colours in polychrome ceramics. The dominant decorative allusion is to Saint George and the Dragon. With a little imagination, the tile roof evokes the back of the dragon, and the bone-coloured parapets of the balconies suggest the skulls of its victims. After dark, brilliantly illuminated, it takes on the air of a fairytale house! *Open*: by arrangement, tel: 204 5250. *Metro*: Passeig de Gràcia. *Bus*: 100 (Stop 2).

◆◆
CASA DE LA CIUTAT
Plaça de Sant Jaume
The City Hall, or Ajuntament, has a neoclassical main façade. The original Flamboyant Gothic façade faces on to Carrer de la Ciutat. Inside are statues, richly decorated halls, a sweeping staircase and a grand courtyard. The Saló de Cent (Hall of the Hundred), meeting-place of Catalunya's leading notables, dates from the 14th century. The paintings by Josep M Sert in the Saló de Crónicas chronicle a Catalan expedition to the Far East in the 14th century. *Metro*: Jaume I, Liceu, Plaça de Catalunya. *Bus*: 100 (stop 15).

◆◆◆
CASA LLEÓ-MORERA
Passeig de Gràcia 35
This apartment building was completed by Domènech i Montaner in 1905, with contributions from leading sculptors, glaziers, joiners, painters and mosaic artists. They elaborately decorated the first floor apartment for the

family that owned the building. This work has been carefully refurbished and the first floor is now the headquarters of the Patronat Municipal de Turisme.
Open: Monday to Saturday 09.00–14.30 and 15.30–17.30hrs.
Metro: Passeig de Gràcia.
Bus: 100 (stop 2).

♦♦
CASA MACAYA
Passeig de Sant Joan 106
A 1901 mansion by Puig i Cadalfach, the Casa Macaya has been converted to serve as the Centre Cultural de la Fundació Caixa de Pensions, and stages many good exhibitions and performances. The covered stairway is especially attractive, and the decorations include some notable sculpture.
Open: Tuesday to Saturday 11.00–14.00 and 16.00–20.00hrs; Sunday and holidays 10.00–15.00hrs.
Metro: Verdaguer.

Casa Milà, a wonderful carbuncle

♦♦♦
CASA MILÀ
Passeig de Gràcia 92
Casa Milà is a big apartment building, which was Gaudí's last work of civil architecture It was completed in 1910 and is better known as La Pedrera (the Stone Quarry) for the undulating mass of rough-chipped stone on its extensive façade. In 1984 UNESCO declared it to be a World Heritage Site. The Caixa de Catalunya, which now owns La Pedrera, has made it the headquarters of its cultural foundation. The building displays extraordinary innovation in its functional plan, the use of natural form and the combination of different materials. Gaudí made prolific use of wrought iron, and *trencadís* (broken marble) was ingeniously employed in the decoration of the four spiral columns which dominate the rooftop terrace. In order to have freedom in the layout of apartments on the five floors, Gaudí devised a method of

minimising load-bearing walls and supporting the building on stone and brick columns combined with a web of steel. One of the interior patios is elliptical, the other circular. Spiral staircases lead from them to the floors and terrace. There are guided tours of the patios and terrace which last about 30 minutes.

Open: guided visits only from Tuesday to Saturday 10.00 and 11.00hrs, noon and 13.00hrs. Visiting groups are very small (maximum 15) and should be booked well in advance. Visits are only to the roof garden. *Closed*: Sunday to Monday and public holidays. *Metro*: Passeig de Gràcia, Diagonal. *Bus*: 100 (stop 2).

◆

CASA MUSEU GAUDÍ

Parc Güell

Gaudí was not the architect of this house, but he lived in it from 1906 to 1926. It now exhibits mementos, furniture and drawings by the architect. See separate entry (page 56) for Park Güell itself.
Open: Sunday to Friday 10.00–14.00 and 16.00–18.00hrs (to 19.00hrs April to October). *Metro*: Lesseps.
Buses: 24 and 100 (stop 4).

◆◆◆
CATEDRAL (LA SEU) ✓

Plaça de la Seu

It was not until 1892 that the principal façade of La Seu, Barcelona's cathedral, was completed. The site first had an Early Christian basilica, then a Romanesque church of which

remains were incorporated into the present building. Although construction of the Gothic cathedral first started in 1298, most of the present building dates from the 14th century. The interior gives a great feeling of space with three high-vaulted naves, typical of the Catalan Gothic style. There are 29 side chapels, some of which are richly decorated. One contains the Christ of Lepanto, used as the figurehead on the flagship of the fleet which defeated the Turks in the great sea battle of 1571. The choir shows fine medieval and Renaissance craftmanship in wood and marble.

In the crypt is the chapel of Santa Eulalia, one of the city's patron saints, to whom the cathedral is dedicated. Her sarcophagus is sculpted in alabaster, the work of an Italian artist in the 14th century. The cloister is a serene place where vaulted galleries enclose a garden with geese and a pond. *Ou com balla*, the dancing egg, bounces on the jet of a Gothic fountain in one of the chapels off the cloister; other chapels display Gothic or baroque decoration.

Most notable of the exhibits in the **Museu Capitular** (cathedral museum) are a *Pietá* from the 15th century, a Gothic tabernacle and the throne of King Martin I, which is used during Corpus Christi processions.
Open: daily 08.00–13.30 and 16.00–18.45hrs; museum: daily 11.00–13.00hrs. *Metro*: Jaume I, Liceu, Plaça de Catalunya. *Bus*: 100 (stops 1 and 15).

La Seu's soaring Gothic nave

CENTRE D'ART SANTA MÒNICA
La Rambla 7
Exhibitions of work in all sorts of art forms are presented in this modern exhibition centre of the Generalitat's department of culture. Its headquarters are in the 18th-century Palau March on the other side of La Rambla. *Open*: Monday to Saturday 11.00–14.00 and 17.00–20.00hrs; Sunday and public holidays 11.00–15.00hrs. *Metro*: Drassanes. *Bus*: 100 (stop 13).

CENTRE DE CULTURA CONTEMPORÁNIA DE BARCELONA
Casa de Caritat, Montalegre 5
New cultural centre with the city of Barcelona as its main theme. Activities are based on exhibitions and research work, courses and seminars.

Open: Tuesday to Saturday 11.00–14.00 and 16.00–20.00hrs. Sunday and public holidays 10.00–15.00hrs. *Closed* Monday. *Metro*: Plaça de Catalunya and Plaça Universidad. *Buses*: numerous.

CENTRE PERMANENT D'ARTESANÍA
Passeig de Gràcia 55
The Generalitat runs this centre to display the crafts, old and new, of Catalunya – the ideal place to get an idea of what is available and what to look for in the shops. The centre adjoins the prestigious shopping mall of Bulevar Rosa and the Centre d'Anticuaris, which offers a wide choice of shops selling antiques. *Open*: June to mid September: Tuesday to Friday 10.00–14.00 and 16.00–21.00hrs; Saturday 10.00–14.00 and 18.00–21.00hrs; Sunday and public holidays 10.00–14.00hrs. *Closed*: Monday. Mid September to end May:

Monday to Friday 10.00–14.00 and 18.00–21.00hrs; Saturday 18.00–21.00hrs. *Closed*: Sunday and public holidays.
Metro: Passeig de Gràcia, Diagonal. *Bus*: 100 (stop 2).

◆◆◆
CIUTAT VELLA DISTRICT (OLD TOWN) ✓

The old town is the strongest magnet for first-time visitors to Barcelona, and it offers a rich mix of things to see and do. It is the area which once stood inside the city walls or just outside them, and from which the city exploded in growth in the 19th century. Silent alleys in the Barri Gòtic contrast with the bustle of the broad La Rambla, where a multinational crowd constantly parades (a walk along La Rambla, is an essential Barcelona experience). The parade goes on past the statue of Cristobal Colom (Christopher Columbus) and along the new Moll de la Fusta promenade beside the old harbour.
Facing down La Rambla from Plaça de Catalunya, the barri of Casc Antic on the left (northeast) holds most interest for the visitor. It includes the Barri Gòtic where an assembly of grand Gothic buildings, quiet patios, narrow alleys and hidden squares created some 700 years ago remains a beguiling time warp.
Restoration and maintenance has generally been thoughtful and the area has not been ruined by its popularity as a tourist attraction. Try to be around the Generalitat building at noon, when its bells play melodies, and if possible visit the Barri Gòtic again at night when it is floodlit.
Carrer Portaferrissa, leading left of La Rambla, is the principal shopping street in Ciutat Vella, with many good and varied stores. If you are shopping for food, do not miss the artistic display of foodstuffs in the Mercat de la Boquería on La Rambla. There is no shortage of places in which to eat well, from basic budget to elegant and expensive. You can sip a drink and people-watch in the shadow of a church on Plaça Sant Josep Oriol, or enjoy rich chocolate from an old-time shop on nearby Carrer Petritxol. One of Barcelona's leading art galleries, Sala Parès, is also on this little street. Across the Via Laietana is the barri of Sant Pere-Ribera with

Barri Gòtic – a bridge to the past

more places of interest: Carrer Montcada is lined with handsome Gothic palaces that have been converted to museums (see Museu Picasso) or art galleries, like the Maeght. It leads to the 'cathedral of the sea', the big church of Santa María del Mar, which epitomises the grandeur of Catalan Gothic architecture. The surrounding area of El Born has good art galleries and interesting craft shops. Beyond the Passeig de Picasso lies the green Parc de la Ciutadella, a place for relaxing but also the site of the Museu d'Art Modern and the Zoo (Parc Zoològic). Fish restaurants are the main attraction of the harbourside area of Barceloneta. From here the cable cars of the Teleffèric ride high across the harbour to the hill of Montjuïc.

Passeig de Gràcia cuts a swathe

◆◆◆
EIXAMPLE DISTRICT

'Eixample' means extension, and this district was laid out according to Ildefons Cerdà's plan for the extension of the city in 1859, controversial at the time and not universally liked since. His brief was to join the old city to the separate municipal areas of Gràcia, Sant Gervasi, Sarrià and Sants. He planned a rigid grid of parallel streets 65 feet (20m) wide in which only two sides of each block would have buildings and the other two sides would be open to a central garden. The cut-off corners of intersections (*chaflanes*) were also to have been open spaces. In fact, buildings were raised on all sides of the blocks, so that the Eixample is very short of green spaces today. The monotony of the grid is broken by broader avenues like Gran Via de les Corts Catalanes and Avinguda

Diagonal. Passeig de Gràcia, three times the width of the Eixample's other streets, is the grandest of the city's boulevards. Parallel to Gràcia is the Rambla de Catalunya with its attractive central walkway and open-air cafés. The part of the Eixample which holds most interest for visitors lies between Gran Via de les Corts Catalanes, Diagonal and the parallels of Carrer Muntaner and Passeig de Sant Joan – mostly the barri of Dreta de l'Eixample. Just beyond Passeig de Sant Joan to the north is the barri of Sagrada Família with Gaudí's unfinished cathedral as its centrepiece. At the end of the handsome Avinguda Gaudí is Domènech i Montaner's largest Modernist legacy, the Hospital de la Santa Creu i Sant Pau.

The Eixample is studded with many jewels of Modernist architecture: brightest of all is Gaudí's Casa Milà on Passeig de Gràcia; also here – the south block between Carrers Consell de Cent and d'Aragó – is the Manzana de Discordia, with work by the three leading Modernist architects (see **Casa Amatller**, page 35).

On the next block, between Aragó, and València, visit the Bulevar Rosa mall, Centre Permanent d'Artesanía and Centre d'Anticuaris, for a taste of the Eixample's many good shopping opportunities. The Vinçon store has modern design at fair prices; Carrer Consell de Cent, between Passeig de Gràcia and Carrer Balmes, is lined with art galleries; and the Fundació Tàpies on Carrer d'Aragó is a world-class centre of contemporary culture. For eating and drinking, the Eixample offers every choice, including lots of *granjes* for sandwiches and salads, pizzerias and pastry shops along Rambla de Catalunya. At night, when the Passeig de Gràcia is attractively illuminated, avant-garde Barcelona moves into the Eixample's designer music bars and discos.

◆◆◆
FONT DE CANALETES
Rambla de Canaletes
If you like Barcelona, make a point of taking a sip from this 19th-century cast-iron fountain which stands at the top of La Rambla near Plaça de Catalunya. Doing so is said to ensure that you will return to the city. Others say it makes you a true Barcelonan, but that is harder to achieve.
Metro: Plaça de Catalunya.
Bus: 100 (stop 1).

◆◆
FONTS LLUMINOSES DE MONTJUÏC
below the Palau Nacional, Montjuïc
The *fonts* are fountains, which are designed to make a spectacular show on certain days. Accompanied by music and changing colours, they appear to dance, in a routine which lasts for around an hour. The 'performances' take place on Thursday, Saturday, Sunday and holidays in summer, 22.00–23.00hrs; and on Saturday, Sunday and holidays in winter 21.00–22.00hrs.
Metro: Plaça d'Espanya.

WHAT TO SEE

◆◆◆
FUNDACIÓ COLECCIÓN THYSSEN-BORNEMISZA
Baixada del Monestir 9
An exhibition of 72 paintings and eight sculptures here is taken from the most representative areas of the overall Thyssen-Bornemisza collection. It includes Italian and German paintings and follows the history of art from the 13th to 17th century.
Open: Tuesday to Sunday 10.00–14.00hrs; Saturday 10.00–17.00hrs. *Closed*: Monday. *Generalitat Railway*: Reina Elisenda. *Buses*: 22, 64, 75, 114.

◆◆◆
FUNDACIÓ MIRÓ ✓

Plaça Neptú, Parc de Montjuïc
Joan Miró, Barcelonan born, died in 1983 at the age of 90, with a worldwide reputation as a painter, sculptor, ceramicist, engraver and designer.
In collaboration with his close friend, Joan Prats, Miró was in

1975 able to realise the plan of opening a centre dedicated to study and experimentation in contemporary art. Another friend, Josep Lluis Sert, designed the light and open building in which the Foundation is housed. Miró donated a substantial collection of his paintings, sculptures, textile creations, graphic works and drawings. Joan Prats also gave some of his Miró collection, and artists such as Tàpies and Calder contributed works of their own. Besides mounting exhibitions relating to Miró, the Foundation presents exhibitions of leading contemporary artists, lectures, film and video screenings, contemporary music performances and children's entertainments.
The fascinating fountain of mercury, created in 1937 by Alexander Calder for the Spanish Republic's stand at the Universal Exhibition in Paris, is here, and adjoining the building is a recently established garden of sculptures. There is also a library and a bookshop.

Sculpture at the Fundació Miró

Open: Tuesday to Saturday 11.00–19.00hrs (Thursday until 21.30hrs); Sunday and holidays 10.30–14.30hrs. *Funicular de Montjuïc. Buses*: 61 from Plaça d'Espanya; 100 (stop 12).

◆◆◆
FUNDACIÓ TÀPIES
Aragó 255
This contemporary art centre, named after the Catalan artist Antoni Tàpies, opened in June 1990 in a converted Modernist building designed by Domènech i Montaner. Tàpies' work shows his interest in different materials and symbolism, besides reflecting his preoccupation with the human condition. Some 325 of his paintings and sculptures and 3,000 graphic works, executed between 1948 and 1990, are on show. The artist's controversial sculpture, *Núvol i Cadira (Cloud and Chair)* sits atop the main façade. Temporary exhibitions of work by other contemporary artists are held in the additional exhibition space. Artistic and cultural events are presented in the auditorium and library. *Open*: Tuesday to Sunday 11.00–20.00hrs. *Closed*: Monday. *Metro*: Passeig de Gràcia. *Bus*: 100 (stop 2).

◆◆
GENERALITAT
Plaça de Sant Jaume
The palace of the Generalitat, the regional government of Catalunya, is largely medieval Gothic despite its Greco-Roman style façade on the Plaça de Sant Jaume. There is a modern carving of Saint George (patron saint of Catalunya) slaying a dragon, and another St George on the Gothic façade on Carrer del Bisbe Irurita. A passageway runs across this street to connect the Generalitat palace with the 15th-century Casa dels Canonges. The palace's main courtyard, with its open stairway and double gallery, is a very beautiful example of civil architecture in the Catalan Gothic style. The orangery is another attractive courtyard. Two other parts of the palace, the chapel and salon, are named after Sant Jordi (Saint George). The carillon in the palace's belltower can be heard every day at noon.

The Generalitat is open to visitors on 23 April, the feast day of Sant Jordi. You can also visit on Saturdays and Sundays, but a written request must be made at least 15 days in advance. Enquire at a tourist office for more information on visits. *Metro*: Jaume I. *Bus*: 100 (stop 15).

◆◆
GRÀCIA DISTRICT
The atmosphere of a village lingers in the warren of streets within the barri of Gràcia, which has been known for its independent, sometimes revolutionary, spirit. There are cheaper eating places and shops and some night-time venues which are an alternative to the modishness elsewhere. Its neighbouring barri, Vallcarca, has two of Barcelona's most delightful and interesting parks: Modernist Park Güell and modern Parc de la Creueta del Coll, created out of a former quarry.

WHAT TO SEE

GRAN TEATRE DEL LICEU
Sant Pau 1 (La Rambla)

This magnificent opera house, inaugurated in 1847 and once the largest in Europe, was sadly destroyed by fire in 1994. The façade still stands, and over 6,000 million pesetas have been pledged by private individuals and various companies to rebuild it on La Rambla.
Metro: Liceu. *Bus*: 100 (stops 1 and 13).

Homage to the Liceu
Renowned for their attachment to opera and music, the Catalans were much affected by the destruction of their beloved Liceu. By way of homage some form of singing takes place every Saturday around noon in front of the building, with the intention of so continuing until its reopening, scheduled for 1997. With any luck you might come across someone special. José Carreras has been known to perform here!

HOMENAJE A PICASSO
Passeig de Picasso

This tribute of one artist to a greater, Antoni Tàpies to Pablo Picasso, was executed in 1983 as a feature of the remodelled Passeig de Picasso, which borders the Parc de la Ciutadella. It is a curious, provocative creation composed of everyday objects in a glass case, with water streaming down the sides.
Metro: Arc del Triomf. *Bus*: 100 (stop 14).

◆◆◆

HOSPITAL DE LA SANTA CREU I SANT PAU
north end of Avinguda Gaudí

Many visitors to Barcelona never see the city's largest complex of Modernist buildings, some 20 in all, designed by Lluís Domènech i Montaner. Domènech did not favour Cerdà's rigid plan for the Eixample district, and within the spacious gardens of the hospital he arranged his buildings at an angle to the blocks of the Eixample. Many of the buildings have Mudéjar-style design and decoration. You can view the complex from the public areas.
Metro: Sagrada Família, Guinardo. *Bus*: 100 (stop 3).

◆

INSTITUT I JARDÍ BOTANIC
Parc de Montjuïc

The Jardí Botanic has been closed to the public since 1992, when work began on a new garden located in the Parc del Migdia. However, for information on nature tours of Montjuïc Park organised by the Instituto Botánic, contact them at Avenida Muntanyans s/n, Parc de Montjuïc (tel: 325 8050).
Buses: 61 from Plaça d'Espanya; 100 (stop 12).

◆◆◆
LA RAMBLA (LAS RAMBLAS)

La Rambla is the long street running from Plaça de Catalunya to Plaça Portal de la Pau, by the sea. It is also known as Las Ramblas, because it is formed by five linked streets, all called Rambla-something

(Rambla-Canaletes, -Estudis, -Sant Josep, -Caputxins and -Santa Monica). Rambla means 'torrent' in Arabic and that is what flowed here until it was paved over.

A central walkway with plane trees was first made in the 1770s, and by the late 1850s La Rambla had become the city's most fashionable boulevard. It is no longer the most prestigious place to live, but it is the most cosmopolitan and most animated street in the city, with cafés, news kiosks and strolling people providing an endlessly interesting free show. Some walkways, including sections of La Rambla, now have marked cycle paths (one for each direction) so pedestrians must be on the look-out!

(See also **Walks** pages 65–6.)
Metro: Plaça de Catalunya, Liceu, Drassanes. *Bus*: 100 (stops 1 and 13).

◆
MERCAT CONCEPCIÓ

on the block between Aragó, València, Bruc and Girona
Mercat Concepció is a city market, similar to La Boqueria but smaller. The setting is handy for residents of the Eixample. *Metro*: Girona, Passeig de Gràcia. *Bus*: 100 (stop 2).

◆◆◆
MERCAT DE SANT JOSEP (LA BOQUERIA)

La Rambla
Barcelona has a number of good food markets spread through its city districts. This one has been operating since 1836 and is the overall favourite - a huge expanse of foodstuffs of every imaginable sort, arranged in elaborate and colourful displays. Fish, exotic fruit and homely vegetables become art here.

A torrent of flowers in La Rambla

WHAT TO SEE

From early in the morning to the evening, the place bustles with housewives and restaurateurs searching for their needs among the many stalls. There are also bars and eating places for a drink, snack or meal while you watch the scene. El Pinocho, near the entrance, has become *the* place for fashionable revellers to breakfast after an all-night stint at bars and discos. *Metro*: Liceu. *Bus*: 100 (stops 1 and 13).

◆◆◆
MONTJUÏC DISTRICT ✓

Montjuïc is the hill above the harbour on the west side of the city. There was already a settlement here when the Romans arrived, and it became a ceremonial site which they named Mons Jovis, the Hill of Jupiter. The northern side of the hill has been progressively landscaped since the late 19th century, to become a park of more than 500 acres (202 hectares). It was for the 1929 Universal Exhibition that the park acquired its gardens, palaces, pavilions, sports facilities, exhibition halls, fountains and the Poble Espanyol.

From Plaça d'Espanya you can take escalators right up to the Olympic Complex (sometimes closed to the general public for a special exhibition). Alternatives are by number 61 bus, taxi or on foot (by a roundabout road); by cable car from Barceloneta, or from Moll Barcelona in the harbour; by funicular from Avinguda de Paral-lel; and by bus from Plaça d'Espanya. From the funicular station another cable car rides over the beautiful Jardins de Mossèn Jacint Verdaguer and Parc d'Atraccions de Montjuïc (amusement park) to the Castell de Montjuïc. Now dominating the hill more than the castle is the Anella Olímpica (Olympic Ring: see pages 31 and 34). These and other sports venues, and the new INEF sports university, make Montjuïc a paradise for the sports enthusiast. Right by the Olympic Complex is the charming little park Jardín d'Aclimatació, with over 200 species of trees, flowers and plants from all over the world. It has its cultural side too – see separate entries for the Museu d'Art de Catalunya (temporarily closed) and the Fundació Miró. The Mercat de les Flors theatre, a converted flower market, and (in summer) the Teatre Grec offer a variety of good productions. In the Poble Espanyol, anyone with an interest in the architecture of Spain can quickly get an idea of regional and period variations from the reproduction façades of many of the country's most famous buildings. There are also craftshops, bars, eating places and late-night haunts to enjoy. Nearby is the Pavelló Barcelona, a reconstruction of the architectural gem designed by Mies van der Rohe. On Saturday and Sunday nights there is a magical display of the fountains below the Palau Nacional; on Thursday nights in summer, horsemen of the municipal police present their Carousel. At any time there are green spaces for lazing, exercising or enjoying the view.

◆◆
MONUMENT A COLOM
Plaça Portal de la Pau
An iron column of some 165 feet (50m) supports the statue of Cristobal Colom (Christopher Columbus), raised for the Universal Exhibition of 1888. A lift takes you to the viewing platform for panoramic views.
Open: Late March to end May: Tuesday to Saturday 10.00–14.00 and 15.30–20.00hrs; Sunday and public holidays 10.00–20.00hrs. June to late September: daily 09.00–21.00hrs. Late September to late March: Tuesday to Saturday 10.00–14.00 and 15.30–19.00hrs; Sunday and public holidays 10.00–19.00hrs.*Closed*: 1, 6 January and 25, 26 December. *Metro*: Drassanes. *Bus*: 100 (stop 13).

Standing proud: Monument a Colom

◆
MUSEU ARQUEOLÒGIC
Passeig Santa Madrona, Parc de Montjuïc
On display are exhibits dating from the early colonising of Iberia, including Roman pieces from Empúries on the Costa Brava; items of the Talayot culture from Mallorca; and Punic (Carthaginian) finds from Ibiza.
Open: Tuesday to Saturday 09.30–13.00 and 15.30–19.00hrs. Sunday and public holidays 10.00–14.00hrs. *Closed*: Monday. *Buses*: 61 from Plaça d'Espanya; 100 (stop 12).

◆◆◆
MUSEU D'ART DE CATALUNYA
Palau Nacional, Parc de Monjuïc
The Palau Nacional was the principal construction for the 1929 Universal Exhibition, before becoming the city's most impressive museum. Great works of Catalan art are kept here. The Palau Nacional is currently being refurbished and the museum is closed temporarily. Some halls are expected to reopen during 1995, when the museum will once again exhibit its unique collection of Catalan Romanesque art – frescos, painted wood panels and sculptures. Most of the works were saved from abandoned religious buildings in the early part of this century. Bright colours were used in the murals and panels, and both painting and sculpture show Byzantine

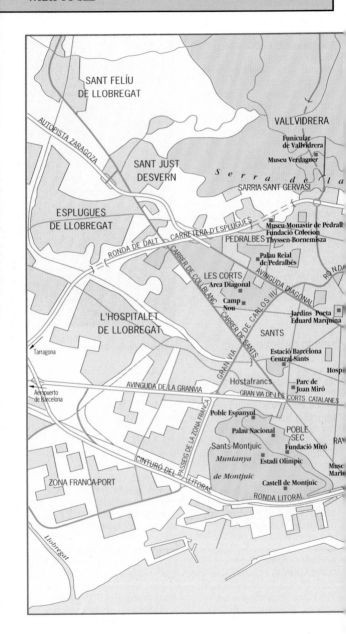

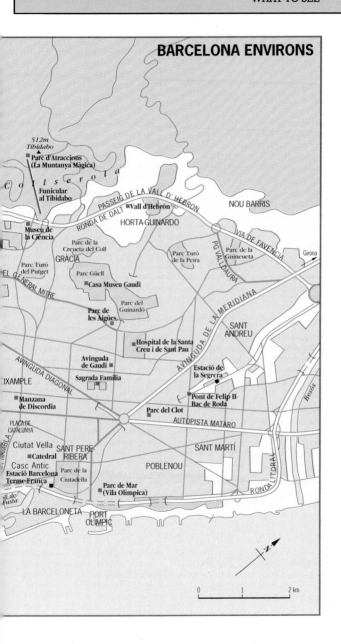

BARCELONA ENVIRONS

WHAT TO SEE

influence in their stiffly poised, neatly arranged representations of people. Beside the strong collection of Catalan Gothic art are Gothic works from other parts of Spain. In painting this period is distinguished by the use of gold for embossing backgrounds (*esgrafiado*) and for raised clothing and haloes (*estofado*). The rest of the museum's collection consists of baroque and Renaissance works including some by El Greco and Zurbarán.
Metro: Plaça d'Espanya.
Bus: 100 (stop 10).

MUSEU D'ART MODERN
Plaça d'Armes, Parc de la Ciutadella
Catalan artists such as Fortuny, Nonell, Casals, Rusiñol and Gargallo dominate this collection of 19th- and 20th-century art. It includes paintings, sculptures, drawings, engravings and decorative art.
Open: Monday to Sunday 09.00–21.00hrs. *Closed*: Tuesday. *Metro*: Arc del Triomf.
Bus: 100 (stop 14).

MUSEU ETNOLÒGIC
Passeig de Santa Madrona, Parc de Montjuïc
Artefacts from many of the world's cultures can be seen here, and the collection is especially strong on those from the Philippines and New Guinea.
Open: Wednesday and Friday to Sunday 10.00–14.00hrs; Tuesday and Thursday 10.00–19.00hrs. *Closed*: Monday. *Buses*: 61 from Plaça d'Espanya; 100 (stop 12).

MUSEU FREDERIC MARÉS
Plaça de Sant Iu
Frederic Marés was a sculptor, traveller and collector extraordinary. The museum was started in 1946 and has two totally different sections. One part shows sculptures from pre-Roman times to the present century; the other section, the 'sentimental museum', has a fascinating magpie collection from daily life, spanning the period from the 15th to the early 20th century.
Open: Tuesday to Saturday 10.00–17.00hrs; Sunday and public holidays 10.00–14.00hrs.
Closed: Monday. *Metro*: Jaume I.
Bus: 100 (stop 15).

MUSEU D'HISTÒRIA DE LA CIUTAT
Plaça del Rei
The museum of the history of the city, in the Casa Clariana-Padellás, is a good place to start your discovery of Barcelona. In its cellars are the excavated remains of buildings from Roman Barcelona, and the exhibits in the museum itself include plans by Cerdà for the city's mid-19th-century extension, the Eixample. Other items illustrating Barcelona's past include views of the city as it was in former times.
Open: Tuesday to Saturday 10.00–14.00 and 16.00–20.00hrs (July to September 10.00–20.00hrs); Sunday and public holidays 10.00–14.00hrs.
Closed: Monday.
Metro: Jaume I.
Bus: 100 (stop 15).

◆◆◆
MUSEU MARÍTIM
Plaça Portal de la Pau
Medieval shipyards called the
Drassanes, dating from the 13th
century, have been well
restored to create this museum
chronicling maritime history.
Pride of place is held by a
replica of *La Real*, the flagship of
Don Juan of Austria, brother of
Philip II, who destroyed the
Turkish fleet in the battle of
Lepanto in 1571.
Open: Tuesday to Saturday
09.30–13.00 and 16.00–19.00hrs;
Wednesday to Friday
09.30–14.00 and 16.00–20.00hrs;
Sunday and public holidays
10.00–14.00hrs. *Closed*:
Monday. *Metro*: Drassanes.
Bus: 100 (stop 13).

◆◆◆
MUSEU MONESTIR DE PEDRALBES
Baixada Monestir 9
Queen Elisenda, wife of Jaume II
who ordered the building of
Barcelona's cathedral, founded
the monastery in the 14th
century and is buried here. This
is one of the gems of Catalan
Gothic architecture. The multi-
level cloister is the best in
Barcelona, with the slender
columns and delicate arches
typical of the period. There are
echoes of past monastic life in
the kitchen, refectory and
chapter house, and the nuns'
church can also be visited. This
peaceful place is outside the city
centre, but is worth the journey.
Open: Tuesday to Sunday 10.00–
14.00hrs (Saturday until
17.00hrs). *Closed*: Monday.
Generalitat Railway: Reina
Elisenda. *Buses*: 22, 64, 75, 114.

◆
MUSEU DE LA MÚSICA
Diagonal 373
The collection of musical
instruments is only part of the
attraction – the museum
building itself is also full of
interest. Puig i Cadalfach
completed the Modernist
renovation of this mansion in
1904. Instruments from the 16th
century onwards are grouped
by type, and there is material
on Catalan composers.
Open: Tuesday and Thursday to
Sunday 10.00–14.00hrs;
Wednesday 17.00–20.00hrs
(except late June to late September). *Closed*: Monday. *Metro*:
Diagonal. *Bus*: 100 (stop 2).

Frederic Marés' collection

♦♦♦
MUSEU PICASSO ✓

Carrer Montcada 15–19
This museum is worth visiting just to see the beautiful 15th-century Palau Berenguer d'Aguilar and adjoining Palau Castellet which house it. But it is Picasso's work that draws the crowds. This is one of the world's two museums devoted solely to Picasso – the other is in Paris. Jaume Sabartes, Picasso's long-time secretary and friend, donated the bulk of the collection in 1960 so that the Barcelona municipality could start the museum. It includes paintings, drawings, ceramics, and graphics, and is strongest on the artist's early years. There are drawings and paintings from his Andalucian childhood and from his teenage years in Barcelona, as well as portraits of his parents and work he did at the Llotja school of art. The most popular and familiar picture here is probably his *Harlequin*.

Arcaded terrace, Museu Picasso

In 1968 Picasso donated a series of 58 canvases based on Velázquez's *Las Meninas*. The museum also hosts good temporary exhibitions.
Open: Tuesday to Saturday 10.00–20.00hrs; Sunday 10.00–15.00hrs. *Closed*: Monday, 25 December and Good Friday. *Metro*: Jaume I. *Bus*: 100 (stops 14 and 15).

Pablo Picasso
Pablo Ruíz Picasso was born in Málaga in 1881 and moved to Barcelona in 1895 when his father took up a teaching position at the Llotja. From 1899 until he permanently left Barcelona for Paris in 1904 he was a member of the artistic group which gathered at Els Quatre Gats café in Carrer Montsió. Santiago Rusinyol, Ramon Casals and Isidre Nonell whose works are seen in the Museu d'Art Modern were leading lights of the group. Picasso's first exhibition, based on themes of Barcelonan life, was held at Els Quatre Gats.

◆
MUSEU TÈXTIL I DE LA INDUMENTÀRIA
Carrer Montcada 12–14
The museum of textiles and costumes has tapestries and clothing from medieval to modern times, and some much earlier pieces too.
The exhibits are displayed in chronological order in three main sections – textiles, lace and garments. There is also an interesting collection of dolls and machinery. As so often, the building alone is worth a visit.
Open: Tuesday to Saturday 10.00–17.00hrs; Sunday and public holidays 10.00–14.00hrs.
Closed: Monday. *Metro*: Jaume I.
Bus: 100 (stops 14 and 15).

◆
MUSEU DE ZOOLOGÍA
Parc de la Ciutadella, Passeig Picasso
Lluís Domènech i Montaner designed the building – the Castell dels Tres Dragons – to be a café-restaurant for the 1888 Universal Exhibition. On the upper floor is a permanent display of stuffed animals. Temporary exhibitions on zoological, biological and environmental themes are held in the lower hall.
Open: Tuesday to Sunday 10.00–14.00hrs. *Closed*: Monday. *Metro*: Arc del Triomf.
Bus: 100 (stop 14).

◆◆◆
PALAU GÜELL
Carrer Nou de la Rambla 3–5
The large mansion was built between 1886 and 1888 for the Güell family and was the first big architectural project in which Antoni Gaudí expressed his individuality. The building is an interpretation of the Gothic style, with Moorish elements. In the narrow street it is difficult to appreciate its scale, but you can see the severe façade, relieved somewhat by the first-floor balcony, the arches of the two doors, sinuous door grilles and the Catalan coats of arms in wrought iron. Inside, the principal rooms are arranged around a central well which holds the main salon. This has both an organ and a closet altar, and doubles as a concert room and chapel. The decoration is rich and varied – marble columns, parabolic arches, precious woods, appliqués of ivory and mother of pearl, fascinating iron work, paintings by Aleix Clapès and fine pieces of furniture. In 1984 UNESCO classified the Palau Güell as a World Heritage Site. It houses the small collection of the **Museu de les Arts de l'Espectacle** (theatre museum), which also stages temporary exhibitions related to the theatre.
Open: Monday to Saturday 10.00–13.30 and 16.00–19.30hrs.
Closed: Sunday. *Metro*: Liceu.
Bus: 100 (stop 13).

◆◆◆
PALAU DE LA MÚSICA CATALANA
Sant Pere Més Alt
The most glorious confection of Catalan Modernism was completed in 1908. Domènech i Montaner worked with sculptors Arnau and Gargallo and other master craftsmen in ceramics, glass and wood to create what must be the world's most

fanciful concert hall. Few surfaces are left untouched – the elaborate decoration drips off the ceilings as well as the walls. Domènech set out to achieve an integration of art forms in his celebration of music, and he achieved it in a densely ornate but harmonious whole. Almost everybody seeing the interior for the first time is awestruck: some find it excessive and tasteless, more fall in love with the place, but few remain indifferent. The narrowness of the street makes it difficult to appreciate the elaborate façade, but it is really the interior which must be seen. Just looking through the glass doors into the foyer will provide some idea of the rest, but undoubtedly the best time to experience it is during a concert, when the whole place takes on a vibrant

atmosphere. The Palau opened with performances by the Berlin Philharmonic, and has been graced by the world's leading orchestras, choirs and soloists ever since.

Visits by arrangement. *Closed*: August. *Metro*: Urquinaona.

◆
PALAU REIAL DE PEDRALBES
Avinguda Diagonal 686
The city commissioned the Italian Renaissance-style palace and gave it, with the extensive park, to King Alfonso XIII in the 1920s. It is packed with fine furniture, paintings, sculptures and royal memorabilia, and also houses the **Museu Ceramica** and **Museu d'Arts Decoratives**. The park includes a formal garden.

Open: Tuesday to Sunday 10.00–14.00hrs. *Closed*: Monday. *Metro*: Palau Reial. *Buses*: 7, 75, 100 (stop 7).

Green peace in Parc de la Ciutadella

PALAU DE LA VIRREINA
La Rambla 99
'La Virreina' refers to the wife of the Viceroy of Peru. She was fortunate to enjoy the rococo palace which her husband had commissioned, but he died soon after its completion in 1778. The headquarters of the Ajuntament's department of culture, there are exhibition rooms with changing shows, and a shop selling books, posters and cards. Tickets for municipally sponsored shows and events may be bought here. *Open*: Tuesday to Saturday 11.00–21.00hrs; Sunday 11.00–15.00hrs. *Metro*: Liceu. *Bus*: 100 (stop 1).

PARC DE LA CIUTADELLA
Passeig de Picasso, Passeig de Pujades
The name of the park is derived from the huge fort built by Felipe V, demolished and replaced with gardens designed by Josep Fonseré in 1873. The Catalan Parliament and the **Museu d'Art Modern** (see page 50) now occupy the fort's arsenal building. As principal site for the Universal Exhibition of 1888 the park received additional buildings, such as Domènech i Montaner's Castell dels Tres Dragons. The French landscape designer Forestier laid out the Plaça d'Armes, where you can see the beautiful *El Desconsol* sculpture by the Modernist Josep Llimona. Other things to look out for are the Umbracle, a structure of wood and iron now filled with tropical plants, and the steel and glass Hivernacle, which is used for exhibitions.

The monumental fountain was designed by Fonseré, but is more famous today because the young Gaudí worked on its construction. The northeast corner of the park is occupied by the **Zoo** (see page 65). *Metro*: Arc del Triomf, Barceloneta. *Bus*: 100 (stop 14).

PARC DEL CLOT
East of Plaça de les Glòries Catalanes
An old railway site has been imaginatively converted by the architects Dani Freixes and Vicenç Miranda. Remnants of the walls, arches and tall chimney of the railway roundhouse which occupied most of the site have been incorporated into the park's design. The *clot* (hole) has become a playing field, and there are various other pleasing features, such as a bridge walkway, a pergola, trellises and sculpture by Bryan Hunt. *Metro*: Clot.

◆◆◆
PARC DE LA CREUETA DEL COLL
Passeig Mare de Déu del Coll
La Creueta was a quarry in the lower folds of the Collserola hills, and has been converted into a leisure park by architects David Mackay and Josep Martorell. It has a lake with an artificial beach which is used for swimming in the summer, and in winter there are boats for hire. Paths run through woods with viewing points across the city, and inevitably sculpture is an important feature. The large piazza has a suspended sculpture by the Basque

Eduardo Chillida, *Elogi de l'Aigua* (*In Praise of Water*), and there are others by Ellsworth Kelly and Roy Lichtenstein. *Metro*: Penitents. *Bus*: 100 (stop 5).

◆◆◆
PARC DE L'ESPANYA INDUSTRIAL
adjoining Estació Sants
This is a concrete park, created on the site of an old textile factory. The design by architects Luis Peña Ganchegui and Francesc Rius i Camps was controversial when unveiled in 1982, and became even more so when the public were admitted three years later. At first sight the upper level of the park is intimidating and reminiscent of a prison: there are 10 tall towers with spotlights and viewing platforms which look like sentry posts. A softer image takes over on the lower level, which has a lake, lawns, paths, trees and a variety of sculptures (from classical to avant-garde) by leading Catalan artists. Andrés Nagel created the fun sculpture of *Drac de Sant Jordi* (*St George's Dragon*), much appreciated by children.. *Metro*: Sants. *Bus*: 100 (stop 9).

◆◆◆
PARC GÜELL ✓

d'Olot
Gaudí's patron Eusebi Güell had the original idea for the park: it was to be an English-style garden suburb, which would have had 60 residences. Only two houses were built, however, as the project failed, and the property was taken over by the

municipality in 1923. Gaudí's contribution between 1900 and 1914 was to design and direct the construction of the infrastructure, and he did so in his unmistakable style. Sinuous lines and natural forms, mythological allusions, broken marble, spiral-shaped towers and giant lizards are all used here. It was clearly his intention that the constructions – stairways, viaducts, ramps and buildings – should have an organic look. The best bit is the three-tiered construction which he created for a water cistern, with what was to have been the market place above it and a large plaça above that. The hall for the marketplace has 84 columns, based on a Classical style but eccentric, supporting decorative domes. Gaudí's plan was that water would drain from the plaça down the interior of the columns to the cistern – an example of his innovative technical solutions. A serpentine balustrade and bench defines the limits of the plaça, from which there are wide views across the city. Gaudí's collaborator, Josep Jujol, was largely responsible for this bench, which is one of the city's most photographed images. The park was declared a World Heritage Site by UNESCO in 1984.
Open: March and October 10.00–19.00hrs; April and September 10.00–20.00hrs; May to August 10.00–21.00hrs; November to February 10.00–18.00hrs. (See also Casa Museu Gaudí, page 37.)
Metro: Vallcarca. *Buses*: 24, 25, 100 (stop 4).

◆
PARC DE JOAN MIRÓ
Tarragona, Aragó
This small park is popular with local people. Visitors come to see the elevated concrete area with its bright and suggestive sculpture by Joan Miró, *Dona i Ocell* (*Woman and Bird*), which rises to 70 feet (22m).
Metro: Sants, Tarragona or Plaça d'Espanya. *Bus*: 100 (stop 9).

◆
PARC DEL POETA EDUARD MARQUINA
Avinguda Pau Casals
Also known as Turó Parc, it makes a good place to relax awhile in this uptown district. Attractions include formal gardens, children's playgrounds and an open-air theatre, plus sculptures by Catalans, including a monument at the entrance in memory of cellist Pau Casals.
Buses: 7, 66

◆◆◆
PAVELLÓ BARCELONA
Avinguda del Marqués de Comillas, Montjuïc
The Bauhaus architect Mies van der Rohe designed this plain and simple building as the German pavilion for the Universal Exhibition of 1929. Although it is widely regarded as one of the classic buildings of this century it was taken down and had to be reconstructed in the mid-1980s. Marble, onyx, chrome plate and glass were the materials used, and there is a copy of a bronze by Georg Kolbe.
Metro: Plaça d'Espanya. *Bus*: 100 (stop 10).

Parc Güell, Gaudí's suburban dream

◆
PEDRALBES DISTRICT
This barri of luxury housing has one of Barcelona's unsung glories: the 14th-century **Museu Monestir de Pedralbes** (see page 51), which strongly evokes the glory of medieval Barcelona. Pedralbes also has the Palau Reial and, with the barri of Les Corts across Avinguda Diagonal, the campus of Barcelona's university.

◆◆
PLAÇA DE CATALUNYA
Everyone arrives at this square sooner or later in their time in Barcelona. It is the connecting hub between the Ciutat Vella and the Eixample, and is also

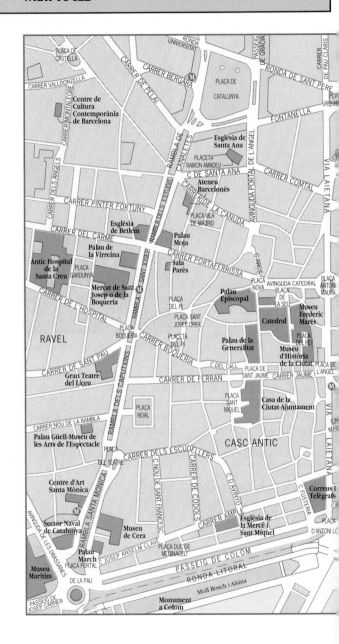

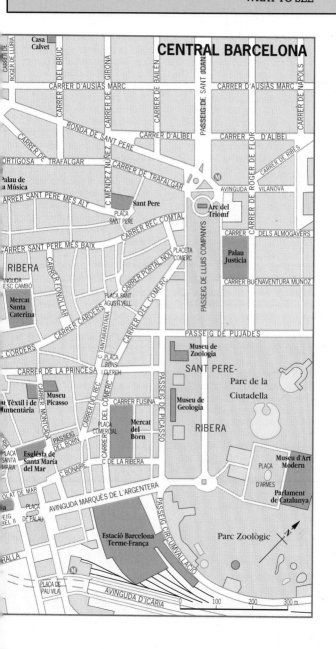

CENTRAL BARCELONA

the centre of the city's transport network – for example, this is the starting point (stop 1) for the Bus Turìstic, (Bus 100.) It is also a venue for public entertainments, meetings and rallies. The plaça as you see it today was completed in 1927. Notable among its statues are two on the western side, by Clará and Gargallo, *La Diosa* and *El Pastor Tocando el Caramillo* respectively. Ornate lampstands are another feature, and some people consider the star in the central pavement to represent the centre of Catalunya. If you want to rest and reflect after a hard session of sightseeing, rent a *cadira de lloquer* (chair) and watch the world go by.
Metro: Plaça de Catalunya.
Bus: 100 (stop 1).

◆
PLAÇA PAISOS CATALANS
in front of Estació Sants
This is one of the *espais urbans* (urban spaces) which leave many people bemused. Architects Piñon, Viaplana and Miralles came up with a bold plan to deal with a difficult space – they unexpectedly filled it with unusual structures. There is a serpentine pagoda, a broad, tall canopy, podiums without statues, a series of fountains, a play area for children ... and more still.
Metro: Sants.
Bus: 100 (stop 9).

◆◆◆
PLAÇA DEL REI
Barri Gòtic
The first sight of this noble square is unforgettable – it can

hardly have changed since medieval times, when the city was at the height of its power. In fact, the 17th-century Casa Clariana-Padellás, on the right as you enter the plaça is a newcomer moved stone by stone from elsewhere and rebuilt to complete the scene. It houses the **Museu d'Història de la Ciutat** – the fascinating museum of the history of the city – (see page 50) and its terrace gives a good view of the old buildings. A wide semicircle of steps leads to the 14th-century Capel de Santa Agueda which forms the right side of the plaça. The chapel's interior has recently been restored and its prize possession is an altarpiece, the *Condestable*, by Jaume Huguet. The same steps give access to the Palau Real Mayor, an enlargement of what used to be the residence of the Counts of Barcelona, which forms the top of the plaça. The exterior has tall double arches and recessed windows and you can see Rei Martí, a 16th-century tower, rising behind. Inside is the lofty, handsome Saló del Tinell, where once the Spanish Inquisition sat and where today a variety of exhibitions and other events is held.
The fourth side of the plaça is formed by the Catalan Gothic façade of the Palau del Lloctinent, built in 1549 for the representative in Catalunya of the king in Madrid. During warmer months, the Plaça del Rei is a venue for musical and theatrical events.
Metro: Jaume I.
Bus: 100 (stop 15).

The Columbus Connection

It was in the Saló del Tinell that Christopher Columbus is said to have been received by the Catholic Kings when he returned from his first discovery voyage of America in 1493. Accompanied by a few natives and armed with ornaments and plants, he was widely acclaimed as a hero. Although Catalunya had played a significant role in the venture, however, it was not to benefit from it and the rising fortunes of the southern ports of Sevilla and Cadiz saw the decline of Barcelona as a great seaport, while the rewards were reaped by the crown of Castile.

◆ PLAÇA REIAL

off La Rambla

The rectangle of neoclassical arcaded buildings was built in the last century, on the site of Barcelona's Capuchin convent. Having acquired a very sleazy reputation, it has now been restored to its former elegance, but the police are permanently on patrol to ensure that it does not become its old, intimidating self. It retains a certain seediness however. The Plaça Reial is graced by tall palm trees, two street lamps by Gaudí and a fountain showing the Three Graces. Numerous bars line the arcades and their tables and chairs spill out into the open air in summer. On Sundays this is the busy scene of a stamp and coin market.
Metro: Liceu. *Bus*: 100 (stop 13).

◆◆◆ POBLE ESPANYOL ✓

Avinguda del Marqués de Comillas, Montjuic

The *poble* (village) was built for the Universal Exhibition of 1929, and portrays the architecture of Spain's regions by reproducing the façades of notable buildings. The village has been extensively renovated and refurbished and is now managed by a private company with an eye to Catalunya's tourist industry. It is an undeniably touristy place but even the most hardened travel snob could warm to it. Besides seeing the various architectural styles and being temporarily transported to other parts of Spain, you can visit artisan workshops and artists' studios, handicraft and souvenir shops, restaurants specialising in regional food and drink, bars, music bars, nightclubs and a disco. There is also an audio-visual on Barcelona, and some kind of show is usually being presented in the main square.

Rei Marti over Plaça del Rei

WHAT TO SEE

Open: Monday 09.00–20.00hrs;
Tuesday to Thursday 09.00–
03.00hrs; Friday and Saturday
09.00–04.00hrs; Sunday
09.00–22.00hrs
Metro: Plaça d'Espanya.
Bus: 100 (stop 10).

◆
PONT DE FELIP II – BAC DE RODA
connecting Felip II and Bac de Roda
This 420-foot (128m) bridge-
sculpture by engineer and
architect Santiago Calatrava is
one of the most outstanding
examples of Barcelona's *nou
urbanisme* programme.
Metro: Clot.

PORT OLÍMPIC
With its lively open-air
restaurants, bars and attractive
views of the yacht harbour, the
new Port Olímpic area has
become an 'in' place.

PORT VELL
This remodelling of the old port
extends over a large area, with
plenty of space to enjoy its
numerous and varied
attractions. The Moll de la Fusta
offers a pleasant seaside
promenade along the harbour,
with plenty of bars and
restaurants. Nearby, you can
take a short cruise around the
harbour on a 'Golondrina' boat.
The Moll de España abounds
with shops, eateries, bars and
the attractive promenade known
as Rambla del Mar leads from
the Columbus monument along
the shore to the Olympic Village
and Port Olímpic.

◆
RECINTE FIRAL
Plaça d'Espanya, Montjuïc
Barcelona has a full annual
agenda of trade and consumer
fairs, which are held in this
extensive fair complex. Most of
it was constructed for the
Universal Exhibition of 1929.
Some events are open to the
public, and it is always worth
checking what is on.
Metro: Plaça d'Espanya.
Bus: 100 (stop.10).

SAGRADA FAMÍLIA ✓

Plaça de la Sagrada Família
The Sagrada Família cathedral
is the most amazing building in
a city of extraordinary
structures. It was the last and
greatest work by Gaudí, who
died (in 1926) before it was
finished, and left Barcelona with
a controversy which still
rumbles on. Some people argue
that it should be left incomplete,
and that the unfinished building
should become the centrepiece
of a park dedicated to Antoni
Gaudí. They feel there is no
merit today in trying to guess
the ideas of an architect who
died some 65 years ago. For
others, completing the work is a
passion, which ensures that
bequests and donations
continue to provide funds. Jordi
Bonet Armengol, a son of one of
Gaudí's collaborators, is the
project's chief architect and
believes that the undertaking
will be fulfilled.
The cathedral's first architect
was Francesc Villar, who
conceived it as a neo-Gothic
structure, on which work began

in 1882. He partly completed the crypt in which there is now a small museum. When Gaudí took charge soon after, he typically decided to do something completely different. There was to be a central tower rising to some 600 feet (180m) and three façades with other towers and spires dedicated to the Virgin, the Evangelists and Apostles. In his time only the Façana del Naixement (Nativity) facing Carrer de Marina, one of its four towers (Sant Barnabas) and the apse were completed. Now the Façana de la Pasiò (Passion), facing Carrer de Sardenya, and its towers are also complete and the entrance to the site is through this façade. A huge crane and building materials show evidence of grand works projected. There are major plans to cover the principal nave, which can only proceed if sufficient annual funds are received, with completion scheduled for 1997. A new lift in the Sant Felip tower ascends some 295 feet (90m) to a viewing platform, from which there is a sweeping view of the site and city beyond. No detailed plans were left by Gaudí, but his scale model (which was largely destroyed when anarchists attacked the building in 1935) has been painstakingly rebuilt. Apart from the cathedral's grandiose concept, the detail of the sculpture stays in the mind, and the way in which the whole structure conveys Christian symbolism. The integration of decoration into the flowing natural forms of the structure is another of the wonders of this building.

Craftspeople and artists such as the Japanese sculptor Etsuro Sotoo continue to interpret Gaudí's concepts. Not everyone likes the Temple Expiatori de la Sagrada Família (to give it its full name), but it never fails to impress one way or the other. You should certainly not leave Barcelona without visiting and

Sagrada Família, Gaudí's apogee

coming to your own conclusions about it.

Open: daily, January, February, November and December 09.00–18.00hrs; March, April and October 09.00–19.00hrs; May and September 09.00–20.00hrs; June to August 09.00–21.00hrs.
Metro: Sagrada Família.
Bus: 100 (stop 3).

◆◆◆
SANTA MARIA DEL MAR ✓

Plaça Santa Maria
It took a relatively short time (1329 to 1384) to put up what is one of the most beautiful of all Catalan Gothic buildings, built to celebrate the city's wealth and power. The façade is very typical of the place and period, with its strong horizontal lines, big buttresses and flat-topped octagonal towers, but it is for its interior that the church is most

Stained-glass, Santa Maria del Mar

admired. There is a tremendous feeling of space, owing to the height of the three naves and the delicacy of the widely spaced columns. The gloominess of many churches is avoided, as the light filters through beautiful stained-glass windows – the main rose window is especially fine. Concerts are presented in the church.

Open: 08.00–13.00 and 17.00–20.00hrs. *Metro*: Jaume 1.
Bus: 100 (stop 14).

◆
SANTS JUSTS I PASTOR

Plaça Sant Just
This Catalan Gothic church is now fashionable for society weddings. It was once the parish church of Barcelona and Aragón's count-kings, and is believed by some to have been built on the site of Barcelona's first place of Christian worship.
Metro: Jaume I.
Bus: 100 (stop 15).

◆◆
TIBIDABO

Tibidabo, highest point of the Serra de Collserola, is a feature of Barcelona, forming a backdrop to the city. Silhouetted on top are the Temple Expiatori (Church of Atonement), observatory and super-modern communications tower, Torre de Collserol, with its viewing platform offering superb panoramic views of Barcelona. The **Muntanya Màgica** amusement park is a big attraction with the Automaton Museum, Tibidabo Express and Aladino. A funicular at the foot of the mountain takes you up to the summit.

ZOO

Parc de la Ciutadella
The zoo houses some 7,000 members of around 500 species, from killer whales to the tiniest primates. Floc de Neu, the only albino gorilla in captivity, steals the show.
Open: summer 09.30–19.30hrs; winter 10.00–17.00hrs.
Metro: Arc del Triomf, Barceloneta. *Bus*: 100 (stop 14).

WALKS IN BARCELONA

The outlines of three walks are suggested here. All of them are in interesting areas, with plenty of potential for detours and adaptations . Without allowing for time spent visiting places of interest or for shopping and refreshments, each of the walks will take less than two hours. Places shown in **bold** type are more fully described in the preceding individual entries. The three walks all start at **Plaça de Catalunya**.

WALK 1: LA RAMBLA

A few metres down on the right from Plaça de Catalunya is the **Font de Canaletes** which gives its name to this part of **La Rambla**. Groups gather around here for conversation, and people rent chairs to sit and watch the passing scene. The newspaper kiosks are open almost all the time and sell a wide selection from the foreign press. Note the Modernist decoration on the outside of the old pharmacy on the corner of Carrer Bonsuccés, and peep into the interior. Between this street and Carrer del Carme

you are on the Rambla dels Estudis, named after a university which existed here until the early 18th century. Stalls sell a variety of caged birds, small animals and fish. Turn right down Carrer del Carme, past the 17th-century baroque façade of the Església de Betlem. You can go into the courtyards of the **Antic Hospital de la Santa Creu** on the left; and stroll through so that you come out on Carrer de l'Hospital. Turn left, and when you reach La Rambla (here known as Rambla Sant Josep), turn left again. This section is also called the Rambla de les Flors because colourful flower stalls line the central walkway. The highlights of this stretch are the **Mercat de Sant Josep** and the **Palau de la Virreina**, both on your left. Cross La Rambla and note the neoclassical Palau Moja, headquarters of the Generalitat's Department of Culture and one of the remaining examples of fine palaces built during the 18th century. As you go into Carrer Portaferrissa, look out for the decorative fountain. This is the principal street for fashion shopping in the Ciutat Vella. Turn right into Carrer Petrixol, which is lined with art galleries and *granjes* serving delectable sweet goodies, coffee and chocolate. The street leads to the small Plaça del Pi, scene of an antiques market on Thursday, and of a 15th-century Gothic church with a magnificent rose window. Leave the plaça by walking through the shopping mall of Galeries Maldà. Back on Portaferrissa, go right to the Plaça Cucurulla where pavement artists are often at work. Turn right again down narrow Carrer del Pi to the attractive Plaça Sant Josep Oriol. An art and craft market is held here at weekends. Leave by the tiny Plaçeta del Pi on to Carrer Boqueria, and turn right towards the Plaça de Boqueria on La Rambla. Up on the right, a Chinese dragon decorates the Casa Bruno Quadras, by the Modernist architect Josep Vilaseca. The umbrella motifs indicate that an umbrella shop originally occupied the ground floor. The ceramic tile decoration on La Rambla's central pavement was designed by Joan Miró. On the other side of La Rambla, note the Modernist exterior of the Antigua Casa Figueras. As you head on towards the sea you are on the Rambla dels Caputxins and the empty façade of the **Gran Teatre del Liceu** is on your right. In the warmer months the old-style Café de la Opera and other café bars operate along the centre. Go left into the **Plaça Reial** and when leaving it cross La Rambla to see Gaudí's **Palau Güell**. Back on La Rambla, turn right. The big Teatre Principal is on your right, and opposite on the Plaça del Teatre is the *Pitarra*, a Modernist memorial to Frederic Soler, who is regarded as the father of modern Catalan theatre. From here the last wide stretch is called Rambla Santa Mònica, which is the least salubrious part of La Rambla. On the right-hand side is the **Centre d'Art Santa Mònica** and opposite is the Palau March, another survivor of the 18th-century palaces which once graced La Rambla. Down a passageway on the left is the Museu de Cera (wax museum – see under **Children**, page 105). La Rambla ends in the hopefully named Plaça Portal de la Pau (Gate of Peace) from which the **Monument a Colom** rises. Towards the right is the entrance to the **Museu Marítim**. From here you could continue left on to the Moll de la Fusta, for refreshments overlooking the harbour.

◆◆◆
WALK 2: THE BARRI GÒTIC
From the Plaça de Catalunya, start along La Rambla and then turn first left into Carrer de Santa Ana, a pedestrianised shopping street. Look out for the doorway on the left which leads to the pretty Plaçeta Ramon Amadeu. The Monestir de Santa Ana here, with its Romanesque church and Gothic cloister, is an unsung gem of Barcelona's architectural heritage. Leave the same way and take the tiny lane opposite into Plaça Villa de Madrid. On the corner to your right is the Ateneu Barcelonès, a cultural institution which holds good exhibitions in its 18th-century building. Go past the Hotel Villa Madrid, turn left into the small lane, and then right to reach Plaça Cucurulla, then turn into Carrer Boters to reach Plaça Nova. Picasso designed the mural for the modern Institute of Architects building on the left. Ahead is the Portal del Bisbe, whose two round towers, later modified, were built as part of the Roman wall. Just through the portal here is the Palau del

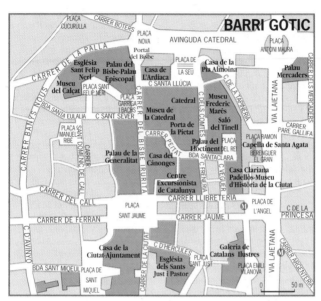

Bisbe (Episcopal Palace), whose fine 12th-century courtyard can be spied through the gate. In the lane on your left, look into the attractive patio of the Casa de l'Ardiaca (Archdeacon's House) with its beautiful Gothic fountain. The house is a 15th-century reconstruction of an earlier building, and now houses the Institute of Municipal History. Opposite is the Romanesque chapel of Santa Llúcia, which has a doorway into the cathedral cloister.

Back in the Carrer del Bisbe, go left into a small square, where it is quite likely there will be buskers performing. Go right down the side of the Palau del Bisbe and note the very old frescos on its façade. An arch leads you into one of the city's most beguiling corners, the Plaça Sant Felip Neri. Concerts are held in the church on the right. Here too is the odd little Museu del Calçat (shoe museum – *open*: Tuesday to Saturday 11.00–14.00hrs). Leave the plaça by the opposite exit and turn left to get back to Carrer del Bisbe. The Casa dels Canonges (Canons' House) on the right was built in the 14th century but has been much changed. On the left the Porta de la Pietat (Door of Pity) leads into the cathedral cloister. The door gets its name from the wooden relief above the entrance. Continue around to the right to reach the doorway to the Centre Excursionista de Catalunya, an influential association of lovers of the Catalan landscape. Inside, columns from the Roman temple of Augustus can be seen. When you reach the Plaça de Sant Jaume, where the buildings of the **Generalitat** and Ajuntament (**Casa de la Ciutat**) face each other, go down the left side of the Ajuntament, noting its original façade. Take the first left to reach Plaça Sant Just, which is dominated by the church of **Sants Just i Pastor**. The fountain dates from the 14th century. Down Carrer Bisbe Caçador, the handsome Palau de Comtessa de Palamós now houses the Galeria de Catalans Ilustres (Academy of Literature and Illustrious Catalans). Leave Plaça Sant Just via Carrer de Lledò, which has examples of the grand houses built by the business community during the city's medieval heyday. Cross Carrer Jaume I, then go first right and first left. You will already have seen quite a few interesting shops on this walk, and there are more in this vicinity. The **Museu d'Història de la Ciutat** is on the right, followed by the captivating ensemble of the **Plaça del Rei**. Leave it by bearing right, and with the mass of the cathedral on your left, you should reach the **Museu Frederic Marés**.

From the Plaça de la Seu you can admire the impressive façade of the **Catedral**. As you look down the steps, the building on the right is the Casa Pia Almoina, mainly 15th century, which housed a charitable institution committed to feeding 100 people each day. Go around it to the right, and follow the remains of the Roman wall to the Plaça Ramon Berenguer el Gran, where an equestrian statue by Josep Llimona commemorates Ramon Berenguer III, Count of Barcelona. There are five well-restored towers and curtain walls from the Roman fortifications here.

If you have had enough walking, you can return to Plaça de l'Angel and join the metro from Jaume I to go elsewhere. To continue the walk, go left into Carrer Salvador Aulet, across Via Laietana into Carrer Manresa, and right into Carrer Argenteria (Plateria) to the grand church of **Santa Maria del Mar**. Go along the side of the church into Passeig del Born, making sorties into side streets which have art galleries and craft shops. The big wrought-iron building of the Mercat del Born, now used for rallies and fairs, was completed in 1876 by architects Mestres and Fontseré. They were also responsible for the completion of the cathedral's main façade. Back near the church, go right into the Plaçeta and Carrer Montcada which is lined by fine palaces. This is one of the most popular tourist streets in the city because the **Museu Picasso** is located at its upper end. It also has the **Museu Tèxtil i de la Indumentària** and interesting art galleries and shops.

◆◆◆
WALK 3: THE EIXAMPLE

Leave the Plaça de Catalunya on the northwest corner into Passeig de Gràcia and go first right into Carrer de Casp. The Renaissance-inspired touches on the façade of number 46 are by one of the lesser-known

Modernist architects, Juli Batllevell. On the corner with Carrer del Bruc, you can see the Casa Calvet, which Gaudí completed in 1900. It shows baroque influences in its decoration. Turn left up Carrer del Bruc crossing Gran Via de les Corts Catalanes and two more streets to reach Carrer d'Aragó. Look out for examples of less publicised Modernist works on the way. (Over to the left on Carrer Aragó is one of the oldest buildings in the Eixample, the 15th-century Església de la Concepció which has an attractive cloister.) Cross to the right over Carrer Aragó and cross the **Mercat Concepció** to the opposite exit. Go left along Carrer València and before turning right into Carrer Roger de Lluria notice on your left the Modernist Conservatori Municipal de Música, completed by Antoni de Falguera in 1914. On the left corner of Carrers Roger de Lluria and Mallorca is the Palau Montaner, by Domènech i Montaner. Domènech also designed Casa Thomas, to the right at Mallorca 291, which now houses the design store, B D Ediciones. Continue along Roger de Lluria to Avinguda Diagonal. Across to the left is the big triangular block of the Casa Terrades (Casa de les Punxes) designed by Puig i Cadalfach. Turn left and one block on is his Casa Quadras which houses the **Museu de la Música**. Almost opposite is the flowery front of the Casa Comalat by Modernist architect Salvador Valeri i Pupurull. Go left into Passeig de Gràcia: from now on the many elegant shops will no doubt draw you to their well-dressed windows. The decorative streetlamps and benches are by the Modernist Pere de Falquès. Gaudí's **Casa Milà** dominates the second block on the left. Further down, on the opposite side between Carrers de València and d'Aragó, are the Bulevar Rosa, Centre de

Plaça de Catalunya is the city's hub

Anticuaris and **Centre Permanent d'Artesanía** (see also **Shopping**). The next block is the Manzana de Discordia, or Block of Discord, with the **Casa Amatller**, **Casa Batlló** and **Casa Lleó-Morera**. Go right along Carrer Consell de Cent, which has several art galleries, and right into Carrer de Balmes. First right and opposite is the **Fundació Tàpies**. Turn right and walk back to the Plaça de Catalunya along the pleasant central walkway of Rambla de Catalunya.

EXCURSIONS FROM BARCELONA

Catalunya is not a very large region, but it has a lot of variety and many areas of great natural beauty. It is also packed with places of historic interest, including some very attractive spots. As distances are relatively short, Barcelona is a convenient base from which to make day excursions. Both the road and rail systems are good and there are organised coach excursions to quite a few places. RENFE the national rail company, and FGC, the Generalitat's rail network, have restored old rolling stock and locomotives (some of them steam powered), and operate special tourist trains to a few destinations.

This is a small sample of the many places worth a visit. Opening times and public transport services are subject to change and are also affected by local holidays, so it is always wise to get the latest information from the Generalitat's tourist office at Gran Via de les Corts Catalanes 658 before planning an excursion.

Montserrat's mountain monastery

◆◆◆
MONTSERRAT

30 miles (48km) west of Barcelona

Montserrat is a mass of sandstone and conglomerate rock with a serrated spine rising to some 4,000 feet (1,220m) above the plain. It can be seen from far away, and makes an impressive natural feature, but it is a small dark statue and its legend which gives the mountain its great significance. Montserrat is the spiritual centre of the Catalan people, with a monastery and a basilica, completed in 1592. The basilica is the home of the image of La Mare de Deu (The Mother of God), blackened by the smoke of millions of candles over the centuries and affectionately known as La Morenita (The Dark

restaurants and shops. Paintings and sculpture adorn the basilica and are on show in the museum, and a boys' choir, known as La Escolanía, sings in the basilica daily (except July and Christmas). Hermitages dot the mountainside and there are many paths to walk, with views far and wide. It is an hour's walk or a short funicular ride to Sant Jeromi hermitage, which stands near the highest point of the mountain.

Montserrat is clearly signposted for drivers from Barcelona. Take the A2/A7 (E4) autopista (direction Lleida and Tarragona), and join the N11 at exit 25, then follow local road C1411 and a twisting scenic drive up the mountain. Or take the train – the FGC service from Plaça d'Espanya – and then the cable car. Enquire at the station about the *Cami de Montserrat*, a combined ticket for train, cable car and funiculars.

One). She is said to have been made by St Luke and brought to the area by St Peter. When the Moors invaded in the 8th century she was hidden in what is now called the Santa Cova (Holy Cave) and when discovered there in AD880 she refused to be moved. A shrine and chapel were built and nuns guarded her until 976, when a Benedictine monastery was first established. It became an influential centre of learning and culture, and many notables visited it to pay their respects to the Virgin. Napoleon's army sacked the monastery in 1811 and it sank into decline until 1874 when monks returned and began rebuilding it. The monastery buildings look more suited to an army but they provide the 300 monks, and their visitors, with modern comforts: there are hostels,

La Escolanía

La Escolanía was formed in the 13th century and is one of the earliest known boys' choirs in Europe. Young boys between 8 and 14 years of age are brought up in the monastery of Montserrat, receiving religious education. Their singing is dedicated to the Virgin of Montserrat and the choir can be heard daily at 13.00hrs in the Basilica, when they sing the Salve Regina and Virolai (Montserrat anthem) with the exception of July and at Christmas. To hear a performance is a very moving experience and the highlight of any visit to Montserrat.

EXCURSIONS

◆◆
SITGES

26 miles (42km) south of Barcelona
Sitges is an old grandee among Spain's resorts – it is one of those which defies the claim that all Spanish resorts are ugly ribbons of concrete high-rises along the seashore. It remains elegant, despite some signs of wear and neglect – somehow these only add to the general charm. Sitges has for a long time been the weekend and holiday playground of Barcelonans, and the smart villas of wealthy families along the Passeig Marítim and in the areas of Vinyet and Terramar include examples of Modernist and *noucentiste* architecture. It has had a reputation for being favoured by creative people since the versatile Modernist Santiago Rusinyol first brought the town to the attention of the artistic community with his Festes Modernistes which he started in 1892. His home, Cau Ferrat, became the meeting place for leading artists of the period. Today it is an interesting museum which contains two paintings by El Greco. Next door is the Museu Maricel, beside the picturesque 17th-century parish church on the promontory, which is the most attractive part of the town. Nearer Carrer Parellades (the main shopping street), Museu Romàntic in the Casa Llopis displays the furniture and effects of a wealthy 19th-century home. North of the promontory is the smaller beach of Platja de Sant Sebastia, and beyond that lie the sports marina and modern residential development of Aiguadolc. A

Museu Maricel in attractive Sitges

palm-fringed promenade runs beside the long, wide and well-maintained beach to the south. In February, Sitges shakes off any winter blues it may have and bursts into the festivities and parades of its colourful Carnival, which draws people from afar. It is also known for its enthusiastic celebration of Corpus Christi (in June), when streets are carpeted with bright flowers, and in May it hosts an exhibition of carnations, Spain's national flower. Throughout the year, though less so in the summer, there are festivals of music, dance and theatre. The tourist office (tel: 894 4700) is behind the Oasis shopping centre, near the market and RENFE station. To get there by road from Barcelona, take the C246 autovia past the airport and through the resort of Castelldefels, from which there is a scenic corniche road of 12 miles (19km). An alternative fast toll road has been cut through the Garraf mountain. Regular RENFE train services run along the coast from Passeig de Gràcia and Central-Sants stations, and take less than 45 minutes.

PEACE AND QUIET

Countryside and Wildlife in and around Barcelona
by Paul Sterry

Although many of the beaches and shores north and south of Barcelona have been developed for tourism, there are still large tracts of rugged wooded coastline left. Travel inland and you will find even more variety: high sierras, arid semi-deserts and the Pyrenees.

The Coast

It is ironic that development to accommodate tens of thousands of tourists has led to many of the best beaches and wetland habitats being spoilt both in appearance and for wildlife. But the steep cliffs survive, more or less unspoilt, and wherever you go along the coast there will be something of interest. Rocky outcrops may be cloaked in

Gulls
Although comparatively few and far between, any gulls you might see are worth studying closely. The yellow-legged race of herring gull will be most numerous, but look out for Mediterranean gulls, which have pure white wings, a black hood in summer and a loud 'cow-cow-cow' call. Audouin's gulls are sometimes seen; they have comparatively slender wings and a thin bill and always lack a dark hood. This is one of the rarest gulls in the world and is only found in the Mediterranean.

colourful native flowers and the introduced Hottentot fig, which tumbles in anarchic jumbles of waxy green leaves and red flowers.

Costa Brava - the Spanish name means Wild Coast

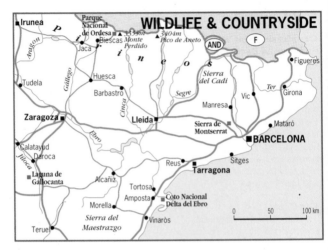

Maquis

Maquis is the name given to the fragrant, tangled vegetation covering many hillsides along the Catalan coast. The scent of rosemary, thyme and lavender pervades the air, and from March until June a dazzling array of flowers is in bloom. Shrubs and trees such as kermes oak, strawberry tree and olive are often found, but the true delight of the maquis lies nearer the ground. Several species of cistus can be found (each with papery flowers and waxy or aromatic leaves), along with tree heathers, species of broom and gorse, and orchids. Insects abound in the maquis: colourful butterflies, day-flying hummingbird hawk moths and shiny rose chafer beetles move from flower to flower in search of nectar. Although the maquis scrub may be largely impenetrable, birdwatchers should not despair. Stand still for long enough and you should see and hear species such as hoopoes – large birds with orange and black plumage and a floppy flight pattern – or Sardinian warblers, small, dark birds with black heads and very distinctive red eye rings.

Woodland

Compared to much of the Mediterranean, Catalunya still possesses large areas of woodland. Along the coast this is largely made up of Aleppo pines, stone pines and cork oaks. Inland, beyond the ridge of hills that border the coast, are woods of sweet chestnut. Along glades and paths among the coastal woods, a rich flora often develops which has many species in common with areas of maquis. Brooms, gorses and tree heathers stand out, with other species such as cistuses, orchids and lavenders adding splashes of colour. The birdlife of these woodlands is also often similar to that found in maquis.

However, in undisturbed areas look and listen for golden orioles – the song is loud and fluty, the bird an astonishing sun-yellow. After dark, you may be lucky enough to hear a Scop's owl, the call of which is a repetitive sonar-like bleep, quite unlike any other bird's call.

Spring Flowers

Although the Barcelona region receives more rainfall (28–31 inches, 700–800mm) per annum than areas further south on the Spanish coast, there is still a distinct dry season from June to October. During this period much of the vegetation becomes parched and lifeless, and visitors might assume that little grows here at all. Return in late winter or early spring and it is quite a different matter: plant life burgeons and colourful flowers greet the eye.

Although some of the flowers are evergreen and can withstand the summer drought, others survive as underground bulbs and tubers. After the first autumn rains, leaves appear and they begin to grow, with many species flowering during the early spring. Among the more characteristic species to bloom in spring are poppies, crocuses, vetches, squills, grape hyacinths and irises. Wild orchids can also be found in abundance in many parts of the Catalan countryside. Members of the bee orchid family are widespread – yellow bee, mirror and bumblebee among them – as well as man orchids and butterfly orchids, their names reflecting their curious appearances. One of the most striking species is the violet limodore, which produces tall spikes of deep purple flowers in shady woodland.

Sierra de Montserrat

The Mare de Deu image in the monastery here draws many visitors. The monastery's setting, amid towering pillars of rock, is

Cistus thrives in the maquis

PEACE AND QUIET

imposing in itself, but the plants and birds of the area also have much to offer anyone with an interest in natural history. Montserrat is 30 miles (48km) from Barcelona. Take the N11 road towards Lleida and then turn off to Monistrol on the local road C1411.

The Ebro Delta

The vast Ebro Delta empties into the Mediterranean near Tortosa. It is a region of wetlands and rice paddies – home to thousands of wintering and breeding birds. Although much of the delta is agricultural, some of the best areas are now protected as the Coto Nacional Delta del Ebro. From the main A7 road take the 340 to Amposta. From here, one road to the north of the village runs north of the river, while another to the south of the village allows exploration of the southern half of the delta.

Rock bunting

> **Birds of Montserrat**
> *Among the oak and pine woodland and maquis look for these birds:*
> Sardinian warbler
> Hoopoe
> Bee-eater
> Serin
> Woodchat shrike
>
> *Higher up look for:*
> Blue rock thrush
> Rock sparrow
> Rock bunting
> Crag martin
> Alpine swift
>
> *In the sky:*
> Booted eagle
> Short-toed eagle
> Buzzard
> Griffon vulture

The flooded fields, lagoons and drainage canals are among the easiest areas to watch birds, with minor roads and tracks throughout. The 'zip-zip-zip' song of fan-tailed warblers can

The semi-desert of Zaragoza

be heard almost everywhere, and egrets and spoonbills are regularly seen. Flamingos are also often present. Black-winged stilts, resplendent with their black-and-white plumage and incredibly long, red legs, probe the margins for food, and avocets scythe the water with upturned bills.

Reedbeds are not the easiest of habitats to observe, but those in the Ebro Delta are worth persevering with to discover some of their more interesting birds. Warblers advertise their territories with song, and purple herons and little bitterns skulk secretively through the vegetation. Sometimes these birds are startled into flight if a bird of prey passes overhead.

Zaragoza

Inland from the mountains that fringe Spain's Mediterranean coast lie many dry regions with the appearance of semi-desert. Although parts of Zaragoza are now agricultural, there are still large tracts of arid land that are

Birds of Zaragoza

Larks, more than any other group of small birds, find the semi-deserts of the province much to their liking. Short-toed, Calandra and crested larks are widespread, but in a few unspoilt areas, Thekla and Dupont's lark occur. The latter is really a North African species, but has isolated outposts in northern Spain. Other birds to look for include pin-tailed and black-bellied sandgrouse, stone curlews, little bustards and great grey shrikes. Griffon vultures are ever-present in the skies above. They breed, together with a few pairs of Egyptian vultures, in some of the sandstone gorges carved by rivers in the province.

home to some of the country's most unusual birds.

Set amid these arid lands is an oasis of water. The Laguna de Gallocanta, Spain's largest natural inland lake, is a national refuge and a sanctuary for vast numbers of birds. In the winter months, large flocks of cranes arrive, together with thousands of wildfowl and coots. Herons and egrets are abundant and black-winged stilts are one of the most conspicuous waders around the shoreline. The lake is distinctly saline, and has plants more usually associated with the seashore than an inland lake. To reach it, drive to Calatayud, take the N234 southeast to Daroca and the C211 west. The lake shore can be explored along minor roads and tracks running through the surrounding area.

Ordesa National Park

The Pyrenees

If you have a few days to spare, a trip to the Pyrenees provides a complete contrast to the Mediterranean coast around Barcelona. For those on a short stay, the Parque Nacional de Ordesa (Ordesa National Park) is probably the best area to visit. From the comparatively low-lying valleys, full of splendid wild flowers, visitors with plenty of energy can walk high into the mountains, where they will find specialised mountain flowers, many of which are endemic to the Pyrenees, along with chamois and exciting birds such as lammergeiers, wallcreepers and citril finches. To reach the park entrance at Ordesa, drive to Huesca, then take the C136 north to Biescas and head east along the C140 to Tovla. From here the entrance is signposted.

FOOD AND DRINK

Catalunya is one of the best regions in Spain for good food and fine wines, but you can still eat and drink cheaply in bars selling *tapas* (small, tasty snacks) and *raciones* (larger portions).

There are distinct variations in cuisine between different parts of Catalunya. Barcelona has two traditional cooking styles, that of the bourgeoisie (influenced by France) and more filling dishes of peasant origin. But as the regional capital, it has adopted cooking styles from the rest of Catalunya, and in recent times innovative chefs have adapted traditional recipes to make lighter dishes, to satisfy modern tastes and dietary concerns. Catalans cook with olive oil, but have traditionally also used lard more than other Spaniards. Seafood is excellent. Popular dishes are *suquets de pescado* (fish, squid and baby octopus), *bullabesa* (fish soup) and *zarzuela de mariscos* (shellfish in a spicy sauce). Pork (*porc*) is the staple meat and flavours the cooking of other foods. Lamb (*xai*) is especially good, and so are the region's many different sausages and cooked meats, such as *butifarra* and *salchichón*. Pastries are eaten as breakfast or with coffee and chocolate throughout the day.

There are five basic Catalunyan sauces: *sofregit*, a blend of oil, onion, garlic and tomato; *samfaina*, made by adding chopped sweet pepper, courgette and aubergine to this; *picada*, almonds, filberts, garlic, parsley, and sometimes

> ### Catalan Cooking – 'Mar i Muntanya'
> Essentially Mediterranean in character, the cuisine of Catalonia is rich and varied. Its advantage of being able to harvest an abundance of food from both land (or mountain) and sea have earned it the name of 'Mar i Muntanya' (Sea and Mountain), illustrated by the way in which products from the sea and land are sometimes combined in the same dish, such as duck with pears or chicken and lobster.

fried bread, pounded in a mortar; *romesco*, also based on almonds (chefs maintain great secrecy about their recipes for this sauce); and *allioli*, blended olive oil and garlic.

Restaurants catering for the tourist trade have menu translations, but if you want to try other places it helps to know the names of dishes. *Pa amb tomaquet* is bread rubbed with tomato and garlic and seasoned with olive oil and salt. *Escalivada* is a cooked salad of peppers and aubergines, while *esqueixada* is a raw salad of salted cod, peppers and onions. *Espinacs a la Catalana* is spinach with raisins and pine nuts. Pastas are popular and *canelons* (cannelloni) appear on many menus. A popular dish now is *fideuà*, a variant of *paella,* using fine noodles instead of rice. In *arros negre*, rice is cooked in the ink of squid. Fish stews – usually very good – are known as *suquets*. *Escudella i carn d'olla* is a meat and vegetable stew served as two courses. The

FOOD AND DRINK

broth, *escudella*, is served first with rice or *galets*, a broad pasta, and *pilotas*, spongy meat balls flavoured with parsley, garlic, cinnamon and pine nuts. This is followed by the boiled meats, *carn d'olla*. Desserts include *crema catalana*, a caramel cream delight, *brac de gitano* and *coques* (shortcakes).

Eating Times and Places

Breakfast of coffee and a croissant or some *pastises* (pastries) is widely available in café and bars. A mid-morning sandwich can again be had from a bar or café. After an *aperitivo*, lunch starts around 14.00hrs and, as the main meal of the day, goes on until around 16.00hrs. Between 18.00 and 19.00hrs locals have a *merienda*, when pastries are eaten with coffee or a chocolate drink. At home the evening meal is

A feast from land and sea

something light around 22.00hrs (also the best time for dinner at a restaurant).

Restaurants often offer a *menú del día* (fixed-price menu) at lunchtime. In basic eateries this can be fair value for filling food. In more sophisticated places you can do better by choosing from the *carta* (menu). Many restaurants are closed on Sunday evenings and Mondays, and some close in August. The choice of eating places includes takeaways; cafeterias; international franchise operations; tapas bars; and *granjes*, which are milk bars. Or you can go to a market, *xarcuteria* (cooked meat shop) and *forn de pan* (bakery), to buy ingredients for a picnic in one of the city's delightful open spaces.

Wines

Catalunya has eight *Denominaciones de Origen*, or DOs, (controlled wine-producing areas). The best known and largest is Penedés, with Torres the leading producer. Penedés whites are drunk young, when they are light and fruity; rosés are much the same but slightly more vigorous. Reds are light and the best of them, such as Torres Gran Coronas, are well rounded and velvety. Alella, along the Costa Maresme, is the other DO area in Barcelona province, and produces good whites, both dry and sweet. DOs in Tarragona province are Priorat, producing rich, strong reds and sweet dessert wines; Terra Alta (varied wines but in small volumes); and Conca de Barberà (whites and rosés). Girona province has Empordà-

Costa Brava, known for its rosés, and Perelada's Blanc Pescado, a light, sparkling white. Lleida province's Costers del Segre produces good mature, mellow reds. The town of Sant Sadurní d'Anoia in the Penedés area is the centre of production of Catalunya's *cava* – sparkling wine made by the champagne method. The best quality cava is *brut* and *brut nature*.

Other Drinks
Tap water is usually safe. If you have doubts, drink bottled water, *agua mineral*. Coffee is popular, and is served in various sizes and strengths, often laced with brandy. With milk it is *café amb llet*. Rich creamy chocolate is drunk in the morning, for early evening *merienda* and as a nightcap. *Manzanilla* is an infusion of camomile, credited with

Patriotic colours for puddings

calming properties. Ordinary Spanish beer has more than five per cent alcohol per volume, making it is stronger than most European ordinary beer. *Una caña* (from the tap) is usually cheaper than bottled beer. Catalunya produces good brandies: try a Torres Diez Reserva. There is a wide choice of liqueurs and the full range of imported spirits and beers.

Where to Eat
Finding places to eat well in every price category is not difficult in Barcelona, and the following list of restaurants is by no means exhaustive. As well as suggesting specific places, the list leads you into areas and streets where there are other eateries, and gives an idea of the sort of places you can find. The emphasis is on places with moderate prices where you can expect to pay between 3,000 and 7,000 pesetas per person for a three-course meal. Restaurants are first shown under city districts and then briefly described in the listing by type of cuisine. Besides these districts, remember the Poble Espanyol on Montjuïc has a choice of eating places.

In the Ciutat Vella
There are many tourist traps here, but you will also find unassuming, family-run eateries serving filling fare to local people. These are usually best at lunchtime and include: **La Cassola**, Sant Sever 3, in the Barri Gòtic; **Quatre Barres**, Quintana 6, off Carrer de Ferran and near La Rambla (smarter and pricier); **Egipte**, Jerusalem

FOOD AND DRINK

12, behind Mercat de Sant Josep; and **Rodrigo**, in Argenteria off Via Laietana. **Vegetariano**, Canuda 41, is good for vegetable and salad dishes (no alcohol or smoking). **La Pallaresa**, Petritxol II, is a local place, known for its hot chocolate.

See listings by type of cuisine for: **Agut d'Avignon**; **Blau Marí**; **Café de l'Academia**; **Can Majó**; **Los Caracoles**; **La Perla Nera**; **Senyor Parellada**; **Shalimar**; and **Els Quatre Gats**.

In the Eixample

Several places have a good value *menú del día* (fixed-price menu for the day). It is a good idea to scour around looking at menus displayed outside. For local cooking try **Don Pancho**, Travessera de Gràcia 50. An excellent tapas bar is **Moncho's de Barcelona**, Travessera de Gràcia 44-46i.

See listings by type of cuisine for: **Café de Londres**; **Mordisco**; **L'Olive**; **Petit President**; **Los Ponchos**; and **Yamadory-Japones**.

In Sarria-Sant Gervasi

Places like **La Cova del Drac**, Tuset 30 (better known as a night-time jazz venue) and **Can Tripas**, Saguès 16, are lively and serve basic fare at lunchtime. **Taita**, Maestre Nicolau 9, is trendy, a bit pricier and has a pretty terrace.

See listings by type of cuisine for: **El Dorado Petit**; **Flash-Flash**; **Henry J Bean's**; **Network**; **Patxi**; and **Shahenshah**.

Port Olímpic and Port Vell

Newest popular areas, especially in warm weather, are Port Olímpic and Port Vell – where you can sit in or out, over-looking the harbours. At Port Olímpic, try **La Bella Lola,** Moll de Llevant 31 (Catalan cooking); **El Túnel del Port**, Gregal 12 (seafood and regional); and **Don Marisco** (casual, reasonable). Port Vell has **Marina Port-Vell**; **La Gavina** and **L'Emperador**, and on Moll de la Fusta are (besides **Blau Marí** – see under **International) Gambrinus** and **Brasserie del Moll**.

American

Henry J Bean's, La Granada, Granada del Penedés 14–16 (tel: 218 2998). Chicago sets the tone for décor and dishes – hamburgers, ribs and salads. The other 'my kinda town' place, **The Chicago Pizza Pie Factory**, Provença 300, specialises in deep dish pizzas. Both are cheap and cheerful.

Basque

Patxi, Bonavista 21 (tel: 217 2157). A good place to try classic Basque dishes like *merluza a la vasca* (hake) at reasonable prices. Good-value lunchtime *menú del día*.

Catalan

Agut d'Avignon, D'Avinyo/La Trinitat (tel: 302 6034). A traditional place with a famed cellar. Specialities include partridge with grapes, rabbit with almonds and fish with *romesco* sauce. Prices are on the upper side of moderate. **Café de l'Academia**, de Lladó 1 (tel: 315 0026). Rustic décor, classical music, delectable dishes and honest prices. The all-female kitchen team prepare traditional favourites and modern variations. In the mornings, there are very tasty sandwiches. You may have difficulty getting a table at lunchtime – it's very popular.

Can Majó, Almirante Aixade 23, Barceloneta (tel: 221 5455). The smartest seafood restaurant in an area with many similar establishments. The chef's seasonal recommendations, may include *centollos*, delicious crabs from the north coast. The *suquet de peix* (bouillabaisse) is excellent. Prices are on the high side of moderate.

Can Travi Nou, Antic Cami de Sand Cebrià, to the northwest of the centre, in Horta-Guinardó (tel: 428 0301). An 18th-century *masìa* (mansion) beyond the centre is one of the city's top restaurants. In summer you can eat outside on the terrace. Most of chef Josep Mercader's menu is Catalan, both traditional and modern, but with international touches. The wine list extends to 500 wines and cavas. Prices are reasonable for this quality.

Los Caracoles, Escudellers 14 (tel: 302 3185). Go here at lunchtime rather than at night, when the area is a bit rough. The way in is through the kitchen. This genuine and bustling Barcelonan eatery offers good cooking of Catalan and other regional specialities. If you just want something cheap and/or simple, the grilled chicken is a good choice. Other prices are moderate.

El Dorado Petit, Dolors Monserdà 51 (tel: 204 5506). Widely rated as one of Spain's top restaurants, in a suburban

Follow the signs to Els Quatre Gats

villa above the city. Presentation and service are impeccable. Traditional recipes of the Gironan districts of Empordà inspire the *nouvelle* preparation of the best and freshest ingredients. The *menú de degustación* provides delectable, and quite filling, tastes of the house specialities. You will probably not see any change out of 12,000 pesetas per person including drinks.

La Manduca, Girona 59 (tel: 302 3137). The ebullient owner and rustic decoration create a welcoming atmosphere, and the waiters give friendly, attentive service. The cooking is mainly traditional Catalan, and prices are moderate.

FOOD AND DRINK

Mordisco, Rosselló 265 (tel: 218 3314). Simple but imaginative combinations of high quality ingredients are served in a pleasant setting. Try a selection from the salad bar, or go for one of the daily special dishes. Open from 08.30 to 02.00hrs, except Sundays. Fashionable and busy, with budget prices.

L'Olive, Muntaner 171 (tel: 230 9027). A first rate, busy brasserie with fast, efficient service. The *cuina de mercat* menu offers fresh seasonal produce and fish, prepared with flair. Prices are moderate.

Els Perols de l'Empordà, Villarroel 88 (tel: 323 1033). The Empordà area of Girona province is known for its tasty combinations of produce from land and sea, and here they excel at them in dishes like *pollastre amb lagostins* (chicken and lobster) and *arros negre*. A quiet restaurant with reasonable prices.

Els Quatre Gats, Montsiò 3 (tel: 302 4140). The original Els Quatre Gats Café was where artists gathered in the early 1900s, including the young Picasso. The setting is the Modernist Casa Martí building by Puig i Cadalfach. There is art on the walls, and exhibitions are held here; you can also hear live music. Catalan dishes predominate on a menu which is relatively expensive.

Senyor Parellada, Argenteria 37 (tel: 315 4010). Ramón Parellada's family owns one of Catalunya's oldest hostelries, the Fonda Europa in Granollers, and he has transplanted much of its ambience to Barcelona. The innovative dishes are mostly inspired by Catalan and French cuisine. Follow the advice of the patron or his maître d' on what is best from the market that day. Service is very attentive (though the tables are sometimes crammed too close together). Good value.

Set Portes, Passeig Isabel II, 14 (tel: 319 3033). One of Barcelona's most historic restaurants, near the old port. Opened in 1836, it has always

Feast the eye at Los Caracoles

enjoyed an illustrious clientele, offering authentic Catalan cuisine and an extensive menu.

Eastern

Chino Long Hua, Passatge Marimón 6 (tel: 201 8713). Unpretentious, cheap and fairly faithful to the most popular of Cantonese recipes.

Shahenshah, Vallmajor 33 (tel: 209 0927). The decoration and furnishings are in authentic northern Indian style, as is the traditional Hindu cooking of the region served here. The main concession to local palates is a lighter touch with strong spices. Prices are moderate.

Shalimar, Carmen 71 (tel: 329 3496). Pakistani Muslim dishes with *halal* meat specialities; cheap, with take-away service.

Yamadory-Japones, Aribau 68 (tel: 253 9264). One of Barcelona's first Japanese restaurants, and still among the best. An inscrutable chef prepares a variety of raw fish dishes at the *sushi* bar, and there is also a good choice of delicately prepared cooked dishes. Private rooms are available for dining in traditional style. Its sister restaurant, **Yashima**, Josep Tarradellas 145 (tel: 419 0697), offers a *menú de degustación* of eight dishes. Both places are moderately priced, given their high standards.

International

Blau Marí, Moll de la Fusta 1 (tel: 310 1015). Overlooking the old harbour, this restaurant specialises in rice and fish dishes prepared in the new, light Mediterranean cooking style. Prices are moderate.

Café de Londres, Londres 103 (tel: 414 1555). This large restaurant serves classical cooking by Antonio Pacheco, one of the city's best-known chefs. The menu makes use of whatever is best from the market, and for both lunch and dinner the *menú del día* is moderately priced and usually good value.

Flash-Flash, La Granada del Penedés 25 (tel: 237 0990). Modern and efficient with an interesting choice of dishes at moderate prices, this is a favourite eatery of the 'beautiful people', especially at night. *Tortillas* or *truites* (omelettes) and salads are the specialities.

Network, Diagonal 616 (tel: 201 7238). The design is 'neo-industrial' and includes TV monitors at the tables. Dishes include Mexican, French, Italian and some inspired by tropical island food. Prices are fair.

Petit President, Passatge Marimón 20 (tel: 200 6723). There is a wide choice of international dishes and specialities of other Spanish regions as well as the chef's own creations, varying from the most simple to the most sophisticated. Try *bacallà* which is offered in 14 different ways. The service is personal and the ambience almost homely. Moderate prices.

Princesa Sofia, Plaça Pìo XII (tel: 330 7110). This hotel restaurant, on Diagonal in the Pedralbes area, is included here as a place to indulge in a leisurely and moderately priced brunch from noon to 16.00hrs on Sundays. (The **Hotel Meliá-Sarria** offers a similar brunch but the price is higher.)

Italian
La Perla Nera, Via Laietana 32–4 (tel: 310 5646). An attractive restaurant with lots of flowers and plants in the dining area. The Italian chef ensures that the flavours are authentic and the pastas just right. The ambience is friendly and the service efficient; moderate prices.

South American
Los Ponchos, València 196 (tel: 254 0667). A no-fuss, inexpensive place for meats presented in the style of Argentina and Chile.

SHOPPING

For many of its visitors Barcelona's main attraction is its shops, but nobody should come to the city expecting bargains. When Barcelonans smell a market for anything they have or can produce, up goes the price. The most interesting shopping is in quality items of local design and manufacture, traditional craft products and work by up-and-coming artists, all of which Barcelona has in plenty.

Hours
Most shops open Monday to Saturday from between 09.00 and 10.00hrs to between 13.00 and 14.00hrs and then from 16.00 or 17.00hrs to 20.00 or 20.30hrs (food and clothes shops tend to stay open the latest). Department stores and some of the *galeries* (malls) do not close for lunch. Some shops do not open on Saturday afternoon in high summer. Drugstores stay open very long hours or even 24 hours.

Shopping Areas

Ciutat Vella
The old town has plenty of antiques, but there are also shops and galleries offering fashions, art and other items. La Rambla's shops are aimed at tourists: the main shopping area is to the left as you look towards the sea, between Carrers de Santa Ana and Ferran and across to Via Laietana, including the Barri Gòtic and the street of Portal de l'Angel. Portaferrissa is the principal street for fashion shopping, and there are intriguing craft shops in the streets to the right off La Rambla.

Eixample
Here the emphasis is on art, antiques, fashion and design. The prime area is between Gran Via de les Corts Catalanes, Carrer de Balmes, Passeig de Gràcia and Avinguda Diagonal, and also in Plaça de Catalunya, which has a vast Corte Inglés department store on one side.

Diagonal and Sant Gervasi
Avinguda Diagonal has a number of top fashion shops along the stretch between Plaça de Joan Carlos I and Plaça de Francesc Macià. Off this plaça is the fashionable Avinguda Pau Casals, leading into smaller streets with shopping malls where wealthy Barcelonans do their shopping. Via Augusta, Travassera de Gràcia, Balmis and Muntanir offer a variety of shops. Further along Diagonal is another enclave for shoppers, comprising an El Corte Inglés department store and the latest Bulevar Rosa shopping mall.

Specialist Shopping

Antiques

The Barri Gòtic has fascinating antique shops, particularly in **Carrer dels Banys Nous**. **Born Subastas**, Plaça Comercial 2, conducts regular auctions. For old books and prints look in the area of the cathedral and along Carrer de Ferran. Some 70 specialist antique shops occupy the **Centre d'Anticuaris**, Passeig de Gràcia 55, and there are more along **Carrer Consell de Cent**, between Passeig de Gràcia and Carrer de Balmes. **Barbie**, Ganduxer 33, is one of a number of antique shops in the smart shopping area of Plaça Francesc Masià.

Art

The galleries around the area of Passeig de Born are the best for contemporary art. **Metrònom**, Fusina 9, is the leader among them; **Maeght**, Montcada 25, is part of an international group. Barcelona's oldest gallery, and one of the best, is **Sala Parès**, Petritxol 5. More galleries line this street, and do not miss **Sala Artur Ramon** in nearby Carrer Palla. There are many galleries within the Eixample's prime shopping area, but the biggest collection is on Carrer Consell de Cent between Passeig de Gràcia and Carrer de Balmes, where there are respected galleries like **Eude** (278) and **Carles Tache** (290). Nearby is **Galeria Joan Prats**, Rambla de Catalunya 54, with a reputation for good shows. Others include **Arte Unido**, Plaça Gregori Taumaturg 1, and **Tache Editor**, Juan Sebastián Bach 22.

Books, Newspapers and Magazines

Toc's, Consell de Cent 314, is a hi-tech, culture and leisure supermarket, well stocked with books, travel guides and maps, newspapers, magazines, paper and paper items, and music in all formats. Kiosks selling newspapers, maps and guides, magazines and books (some very lurid) are plentiful. Those at the top of La Rambla close only on Sunday afternoon and night.

Crafts

The Generalitat runs the **Centre Permanent d'Artesanía**, Passeig de Gràcia 55 (see also pages 38–9). It displays traditional and contemporary craftwork of Catalunya and is a good place to visit just to see what is available. In department stores and small shops around the city are craft items from all parts of Spain, but a search

The elegant El Corte Galerias

through the Ciutat Vella may be more fun and more rewarding: this is where traditional crafts continue and where the shops are fascinating in themselves. Decorative candles are a local speciality and the best place to look for them is **Cereria Subirà**, Baixada Liberteria 7 (off Plaça de Sant Jaume), which has been going since 1761. There are other candle shops in the area of the cathedral. Ceramic items, including decorative tiles, are another good buy. Start looking in Plaça Sant Josep Oriol, Carrer Banys Nous, Carrer Call and Carrer de la Boqueria; but there are many places, including neighbourhood houseware shops, that sell both rustic cooking ware and finely crafted pieces. Other items to look for include embroidery and lacework, glassware, fans, shawls, *espardenyes* (canvas rope-soled shoes), gold and silverwork, and papier mâché objects. You will find specialist shops in the streets mentioned above, and in Carrer de Ferran, Carrer de l'Hospital and Carrer del Carme on the other side of La Rambla. There are more traditional craft workshops in streets off Passeig del Born.

Department Stores

Barcelona's four big stores are much like those in other countries. El Corte Inglés is considered a bit more upmarket than Galerías Preciados. Both offer tax-refundable purchases, packing and forwarding:
El Corte Inglés, Plaça de Catalunya 14 (tel: 302 1212), and Diagonal 617–619 (tel: 419 2828).

Galerías Preciados, Portal de l'Angel 19–21 (tel: 317 0000), and Diagonal 471–3 (tel: 419 6262). All are open Monday to Saturday 10.00–21.00hrs.

Design

Some say that Barcelona equals Milan as a leading centre of contemporary design; others say Barcelona is less of a leader but is successful at keeping abreast with the foremost trends. You can decide for yourself as you wander the streets and look not only at the objects on display but at the design of the shops themselves (and of restaurants, bars and discos). Your first stop should be **Vinçon**, Passeig de Gràcia 96. This spacious store, which includes an art gallery, has its own design in housewares and the whole gamut of other items. **B D Ediciones de Diseño**, Mallorca 291, has designer furniture including reproductions of Gaudí pieces. **Artespaña**, Rambla de Catalunya 75 and Muntaner 537, is a government-sponsored national chain offering design from traditional to the very latest in furnishings and other items from around Spain. **Inicial G**, Balmes 458, has useful and nonsense items, gadgets and the like, also of the latest design. **D Barcelona**, Diagonal 367, has a gallery specialising in conceptual art, and sells a range of designer items and gadgets.

Drugstores

'Drugstore' in this sense means a collection of shops selling more or less useful things, with a place or places to eat.

The Drugstore, Passeig de Gràcia 71. Open 24 hours every day, it has a supermarket and shops selling books, gifts, perfumes, photo supplies and tobacco, plus a restaurant, cafeteria and bar.

VIP'S, Rambla Catalunya 7. Among its 22 shops, open 09.00–01.30hrs (to 03.00hrs Friday and Saturday), you can find food, books, toys, gifts, paper products, records, videos and photo supplies. There are also a cafeteria and Italian restaurant.

Drugstore David, Tuset 19–21. Open daily from 09.00–04.30hrs, with more than 50 shops. Services: post office, bookshop, food, clothes, cafeteria and restaurant. Reasonable prices and good, simple food make the restaurant very popular.

Fashion
Over the past decade Spain's fashion designers have moved centre stage in the competitive international scene. Look for

Keeping up with the news in La Rambla

names like Sybilla, Roser Mercè, Sara Navarro, Purificación Garcia and others mentioned below. You can also choose from the less expensive models of talented designers who have not yet hit the headlines. Below is a selection of top shops and boutiques; for others try the shopping malls.

For Women

Bebelin's, Consell de Cent 298: elegant, classical designs and famous name collections.

Capital A, Passeig de Gràcia 76: leading Spanish designers are featured, including María Cusata, Gonzalo González and Jordi Cuesta. The shoe salon has the latest designs from Robert Clercerie. Local designer **Lola Barcelò** has shops at Balmes 228, Muntaner 244 and 502, and in Galeries Turò. In the spacious and elegant boutique of **Tema**, Ferran Agull 10, Spanish

SHOPPING

designers like the Madrileños, Manuel Piña and Jesús del Pozo are well represented.

For Men

Furest, Passeig de Gràcia 12, Diagonal 468 and Pau Casals 3, has been a favourite outfitter of the city's more sedate gentlemen for a long time. It stocks leading names from Europe and North America. **José Tomas**, Mallorca 242, is a young designer who has been inspired by Giorgio Armani. A selection of own label and leading names (nothing much in the vanguard) is stocked by **Leoni**, Portaferrissa 13, València 26, Diagonal 506 and 604, and Casp 99. Although the name may sound Italian, **Massimo Dutti**, Passeig de Gràcia 13, Rambla Catalunya 60, Via Augusta 33 and Diagonal 602, is very much a Spanish success story, based on good design, good quality and reasonable prices, all available in a growing chain of shops.

For Men and Women

Adolfo Domínguez, Passeig de Gràcia 89 and València 245, is probably the best-known Spanish designer internationally. The two spacious shops of **Farreras**, Passeig de Gràcia 79 and Diagonal 586, have a wide selection of clothing, footwear and accessories for both sexes and all ages. **Groc**, Rambla de Catalunya 100 and Muntaner 385, sells the creations of the fashion leader Toni Miró. The long-established firm of **Gales**, Passeig de Gràcia 32, Diagonal 490 and 596, and Tuset 1, offers many well-known labels and a selection ranging from staid sophistication to zany youthfulness. Similar in style and merchandise is **Santa Eulalia**, Passeig de Gràcia 60 and 93, and Pau Casals 8. Leather fashions and accessories are the speciality of **Loewe**, Passeig de Gràcia 35, Diagonal 570 and Juan Sebastian Bach 8.

Accessories

Intimo Due, Pau Claris 113. The speciality is lingerie and

El Corte Inglés, Plaça de Catalunya

underwear, and designer labels include those of Conxa Casas and Nikos. **Camper**, València 249, Muntaner 248 and Pau Casals 3, stocks the models of leading shoe designers.

Eleven, Diagonal 466, is a shop of startling décor, where you would expect the prices of the designer footwear to be much higher than they are. In **Patricia**, Diagonal 466, Miquel Mesquida presents surprising designs in footwear and other leather accessories.

Gifts and Mementoes

Populart, Montcada 22, down the street from the Museu Picasso, sells an interesting variety of posters, cards, designs in paper and papier mâché, and ceramic and wood items. Other places to look are **Raima**, Comtal 27; **Konema**, Consell de Cent 296; **La Factoria**, Consell de Cent 412; and **Dos i Una**, Rosselló 275.

Jewellery

Baguès, Passeig de Gràcia 41, in the Modernist Casa Amatller, sells stylish jewellery. The family firm of **Puig Doria**, Rambla de Catalunya 88 and Diagonal 612, has won international awards for designs and jewellery, often incorporating unusual materials. The original designs of **Ramón Oriol** are available at Bori i Fontestà 11; and designs ranging from primitive to avantgarde are the speciality of **Enric Mayoral**, Laforja 19.

Malls

Barcelona has three major new shopping complexes, each of which offer numerous shops,

restaurants and various entertainments.

Located in Plaça de les Glories, at the intersection of Diagonal, Gran Via and Meridian, is the vast **Barcelona Glories** shopping mall, consisting of over 200 shops, cinemas, restaurants, landscaped plazas and offices.

Within the **L'Illa de Diagonal** complex, Diagonal 545-557 (Pedralbes district) you will find fashion and sportswear shops, Marks and Spencer, restaurants and a hotel complex.

The new **Port Vell** development includes a large commercial centre, comprising shops and restaurants.

Other shopping malls include: **Galeries Maldà**, Portaferrissa 22. With 75 varied shops it is the biggest of three malls on this street in Ciutat Vella.

Bulevar Rosa, Passeig de Gràcia 55. The first of the city's malls opened in 1978. Its 102 shops still offer the most central and convenient one-stop shopping. Another Bulevar Rosa, at Diagonal 474, is opposite Galerías Preciados department store and has 39 shops; the newest one, further out at Diagonal 609–15, has 88 shops and is next to El Corte Inglés department store.

Diagonal Center, Diagonal 584. This is a mall of some 60 shops near the Plaça Macià and fashionable shopping street of Pau Claris.

Via Wagner, Bori i Fontestà 17. A hundred shops in the smart shopping area of Sant Gervasi. **Galeries Turó**, Tenor Viñas 12. In the same area, this smaller mall has 30 tempting shops.

Reflecting the look on the streets

Markets
Antiques
Plaça del Pi: Thursday
09.00–20.00hrs (except August).
Art
Plaça Sant Josep Oriol: Saturday
10.00–22.00hrs and Sunday
10.00–15.00hrs (except August).
Plaça Sagrada Família: Saturday,
Sunday and public holidays
10.00–14.00hrs.
Plaça del Roser: last Sunday of
the month, except July and
August, 09.00–14.00hrs.
Books, Coins, Stamps
Mercat Sant Antoni: Sunday
09.00–14.00hrs (books and
coins).
Plaça Reial: Sunday
09.00–14.30hrs (coins, stamps
and postcards).
Crafts
Turó Parc: first Sunday of the
month, except August and
September, 10.00–15.00hrs
(ceramics, glass, enamels, iron
work and textiles).
Fleamarket
Plaça de les Glòries: Monday,
Wednesday, Friday and
Saturday 08.00–20.00hrs

(19.00hrs in winter) – be
prepared to bargain.

Sports
The sports departments of
department stores stock
equipment and clothing from
leading manufacturers. Other
good sports shops are: **Esports
Sanjust**, Canuda 6; **Beristany**,
Passeig de Gràcia 94; and
Sapporo, Calvet 8 (very good
for skiing gear).

ACCOMMODATION

During weekdays throughout
the year Barcelona often cannot
satisfy the demand for
accommodation in the medium
to top categories of hotels, while
in the summer season places
with lower classification get
very booked. Several new
hotels were built for the
Olympic Games, mainly in the
upper category, including the
top deluxe **Arts Barcelona** and
the **Rey Juan Carlos I** hotels.

Many more have opened since, ranging from 2- to 4-star ratings. It is hoped that this will help alleviate demand, expected to increase from both the business and holiday traveller sectors. If you are making independent arrangements for your visit to Barcelona, it is wise to make a reservation in advance. Spain's tourist office in your own country can provide some basic information about officially classified accommodation but it will not make reservations. From the same source, and from press advertising, you can find out details of companies which offer packages of flights and accommodation in Barcelona. A package is likely to be less costly than making independent arrangements, and it is less troublesome. From spring to autumn even cheaper packages should be available to resorts along the Costa Maresme and the lower part of the Costa Brava to the north of Barcelona, or along the Costa Dorada to the south. From these resorts it is easy to make day excursions to the city by public transport, especially by the coastal train services.

Tourist offices in Barcelona, and in the resorts, will provide information about local accommodation, but you cannot make reservations through them. Information can also be obtained from the **Gremi d'Hotels de Barcelona**, Via Laietana 47, 08003 Barcelona (tel: (93) 301 6240).

Spain's long-standing criteria for the official classification of accommodation have now become less dependable, and different regional authorities have applied different interpretations.

The regulations of the Generalitat recognise two groups of establishments – hotels (H) and pensions (P), plus the hotel apartment (HA) subgroup. Hotels are classified from 1- to 5-star, while pensions have 1 or 2 stars. Establishments are now having to adapt to higher standards and simpler classifications being imposed by the Generalitat: all hotels (1- to 5-star) will require a bathroom for each bedroom; in pensions of one star 15 per cent of bedrooms will have to have a bathroom, and in those with two stars at least 25 per cent of bedrooms will have a bathroom. While many places are undergoing remodelling and refurbishing to meet these standards, others – unable to meet the cost or challenge of change – are having to close.

It is advisable to confirm all prices before making a commitment and it is acceptable practice to ask to see bedrooms before committing yourself.

As a rule you will do better booking on a room only basis. Breakfast in a nearby bar will be cheaper and it is an opportunity to be among local people. And with so many good and interesting eating places in the city you do not want to be committed to taking all your meals in the same place.

All hotels and restaurants are required to keep and produce complaint forms if requested. If you are unable to obtain one, you can request it from the Tourist Information Office.

ACCOMMODATION

Hotels and Pensions
A selective listing of hotels and pensions in different city districts follows. Of necessity, the old-style classifications have been used.

In the Ciutat Vella
4-star
Colon, Avenida Catedral 7 (tel: 301 1404), 151 rooms. Combines elegance with a cosy and welcoming atmosphere. Piano bar, modern amenities. Splendid location opposite the main façade of the Cathedral.
Le Meridien Barcelona, La Rambla 111 (tel: 318 6200), 210 rooms, parking. It has recently been renovated to a high international standard and offers the usual comfort and amenities of a top-rated hotel. A favourite place of entertainment stars.
Rivoli Ramblas, La Rambla 128 (tel: 302 6643), 87 rooms. Good design has been applied in creating its gleaming modern interior and it has an excellent situation at the top of La Rambla.

Sumptuous style at the Ritz

There is an open-air terrace and bar with good views. Considering its comfort, services and location, it is well-priced by international comparison.

3-star
Continental, La Rambla 138 (tel: 301 2570), 35 rooms. This is a friendly, well run hotel on two floors of a block at the top of La Rambla. Distinctive blue canopies cover the balconies of its front rooms. Try to get one of them if you do not mind noise and want a grandstand seat above La Rambla. George Orwell may have stayed here when writing *Homage to Catalonia*.
Oriente, Ramblas 45–47 (tel: 302 2558), 150 rooms. Situated right on the Rambla, a stone's throw from the Barri Gòtic. Popular, old traditional hotel, now renovated.

2-star
España, Sant Pau 9 (tel: 318 1758), 69 rooms. Recently

modernised bedrooms offer fair comfort, prices are good, and the location, behind the Gran Teatre del Liceu, is very convenient. Its public rooms have the distinction of elaborate décor by Domènech i Montaner and his Modernist collaborators. Tops for atmosphere.

1-star
Nouvel, Santa Ana 20 (tel: 301 8274), 76 rooms. This old-style hotel on a pedestrian street offers few facilities but reasonable comfort. Rooms vary quite a lot so check them first if possible, or ask for the best room.

In the Eixample
5-star
Hotel Ritz, Gran Via de les Corts Catalanes 668 (tel: 318 5200), *gran lujo*, 161 rooms. Still one of Barcelona's top rated and priciest hotels, and the luxury of its offerings is undeniable. If money does not matter much but superb comfort and elegance do, you will enjoy the Ritz and its touch of class. By international comparison its tariffs are not that exorbitant.

4-star
Condes de Barcelona, Passeig de Gràcia 75 (tel: 484 8600), 148 rooms, parking. At about half the price of the Ritz you get most of the same facilities, similar comfort and a more homely elegance within a Modernist building.
Regente, Rambla de Catalunya 76 (tel: 487 5989), 78 rooms. This is comparable to the Condes, and has a rooftop swimming pool which is an

added bonus during the hot summer months.

3-star
Astoria, Paris 203 (tel: 209 8311), 117 rooms. Very well situated for shopping, eating and nightlife in the Eixample, along Diagonal and Sant Gervasi. Classic hotel, unpretentious but comfortable and efficient with moderate prices.
Gran Via, Gran Via de les Corts Catalanes 642 (tel: 318 1900), 48 rooms. For less than a quarter of the Ritz's prices you can still feel you are staying in a palace. The public rooms have splendid baroque decoration and furnishing. Bedrooms and bathrooms are comfortable and the service is adequate.

1-star
Merisis, Castillejos 340, 30 rooms. This is a modern hotel with basic comforts which is close to the Sagrada Família and Hospital Sant Pau.
Oliva, Passeig de Gràcia 32 (tel: 317 5087), 16 rooms. Old lifts creak to the fifth floor of the elegant block and this simple, family-run *hostal* where all the bedrooms are different but clean and comfortable. Rooms overlooking Passeig de Gràcia.

In Les Corts and Pedralbes
5-star
Rey Juan Carlos I, Diagonal 661–671 (tel: 448 0808), 375 rooms and 37 suites. Super deluxe, built for the Olympics in 1992, with spectacular atrium, several restaurants and bars, gardens, swimming pool and sports facilities. Panoramic

views over city and sea. Convenient for the airport and motorway.

4-star

Gran Derby, Loreto 28 (tel: 322 2062), 43 apartments, parking. Here you have all the facilities of a good hotel – except restaurant and bar – with the advantage of the convenience and extra space of well-furnished and well-equipped apartments.

Meliá Barcelona Sarria, Avinguda Sarria 50 (tel: 410 6060), 312 rooms, parking. This is a modern high-rise building housing an international-style hotel with full and efficient facilities.

Princesa Sofia, Plaça Pius XII (tel: 330 7111), 505 rooms, parking. Similar to the Meliá but even bigger and a bit pricier – and it scores over its rival in having both covered and outdoor swimming pools for the fitness conscious.

Main entrance of the Hotel Gran Via

2-star

Prisma, Avinguda Josep Tarradellas 119 (tel: 439 4206), 27 rooms. This does not pretend to be more than a clean and comfortable *hostal,* and as such it provides a fair-priced choice, convenient to Plaça Francesc Macià.

In Sarria-Sant-Gervasi
4-star

Balmoral, Via Augusta 5 (tel: 217 8700), 94 rooms, parking. Although its compact bedrooms seem a bit overpriced, this is a full-facility hotel and very conveniently placed for shopping just off Avinguda Diagonal.

3-star

Tres Torres, Calatrava 32 (tel: 417 7300, fax: 418 9834), 56 rooms. This is a small and relatively recently modernised hotel, with standard comforts, in a residential area.

2-star

Bonanova Park, Capità Arenas 51 (tel: 204 0900), 60 rooms, parking. There is nothing fancy about this hotel and the bedrooms are compact but it is pleasantly situated in a residential area, near public gardens and a games place for children. For this up-market part of town its tariffs are reasonable.

Vila Olímpica
5-star

Arts Barcelona, Carrer de la Marina, 19–21 (tel: 221 1010), 397 rooms, 56 executive suites, 2 presidential suites. Built for the 1992 Olympics, this is a top luxury high-rise hotel, operated by the Ritz-Carlton Group, overlooking the sea, close to the Olympic Marina.

NIGHTLIFE

Visiting Barcelona and not sampling its nightlife is like holding a bottle of cava in your hand and not popping the cork. The night scene is sparklingly alive with a variety to suit every taste. Live performances range from appearances by world famous artists in every form of expression to nude cavortings which would have made Caligula blush. Music halls emulate the examples of Paris; dance halls are filled with nostalgia for past decades; flamenco *tablaos* evoke Andalucian emotions. Music bars and discos compete not only with the quality of their music and lighting but in the impact of their striking modern design. It is no false claim by Barcelonans that they have one of the most vibrant night scenes in Europe.

Enjoying the best on offer can make for an expensive night out, but there are many venues besides those mentioned below in which you will find good classical or contemporary cultural presentations, be happily entertained or make your own action and fun. Check in the local press, at tourist offices and on billboards. These sources will also tell you about times and where to get tickets. To save time, and money on taxis (advisable at night), try to arrange your programme within a different city district each

night. If you want to enjoy the nightlife at its busiest, go out on Thursday, Friday or Saturday nights, and remember not to start too early: at around 20.30hrs begin a half-hour *paseo*; then choose a cocktail bar or *xampanyeria*; start a leisurely dinner at 22.30hrs; by 01.00hrs music bars are getting busy, and discos are humming at their best from 02.30hrs. The usual starting time for opera, ballet and concerts is 21.00hrs; for theatre 22.00hrs; live performances in bars and discos start between 23.00 and 01.00hrs.

Opera, Concerts, Dance and Theatre

Some important venues are listed below. There are many others, including places where the cultural experience is heightened by the surroundings. For instance, check if anything is on at: the beautiful church of **Santa Maria del Mar** (and other churches); the splendid **Saló de Cent** in the Ajuntament; the evocative **Plaça del Rei**; and the lofty **Drassanes** shipyards. You do not need to know Catalan or Spanish to enjoy the city's rich offerings of concerts, dance and opera. Theatre presentations are predominantly in Catalan but some of the shows, especially comedy and satire, may make sense for those who do not know the language.

Centre Cultural de la Fundació Caixa de Pensions, Passeig de Sant Joan 106. Classical concerts are often given in this splendidly adapted Modernist building. (See **Casa Macaya**, **What to See**, page 36.)

NIGHTLIFE

Gran Teatre del Liceu, Sant Pau 1, due to reopen in 1997 (see **What to See**, page 44).

Mercat de les Flors, Lleida 59. This converted flower market is now a municipally run venue for theatre and dance, where Barcelona's Contemporary Ballet Company often performs.

Palau de la Música Catalana, Sant Francesc de Paula 2. Do not miss a performance by the Orquesta Ciutat de Barcelona or one of the other symphony or chamber orchestras, jazz ensembles, choral groups and soloists from home and abroad: the experience of being in Domènech i Montaner's fanciful creation is as enjoyable as the music. (See pages 53–4).

Poliorama, La Rambla 115. Another theatre sponsored by the Generalitat, where the respected company of Josep Maria Flotats usually performs.

Teatre Lliure, Montseny 47. A theatre which has a resident company doing contemporary work and its own chamber orchestra. The restaurant is very pleasant and popular.

Teatre Malic, Fussina 3. In the area of El Born, where there is a fair amount of avant-garde activity, this is a venue for 'alternative' theatre.

Teatre Nacional de Catalunya, designed by Ricard Bofill's architectural studio, located near the Plaça de les Glòries, and the Auditori, opposite, are both under construction and will be major additions to Barcelona's cultural environment.

Teatre Romea-Centre Dramàtic, Hospital 51. The Generalitat runs this centre of the dramatic arts, offering a varied programme.

Teatres de l'Institut, Sant Pere mès Baix. A venue for theatre and dance, sponsored by the Diputaciò de Barcelona, the province's council.

Shows, Dinner and Dancing

Arnau, Paral-lel 60 (tel: 242 2804). A music hall with good Parisian-style shows, very professionally done.

Belle Époque, Muntaner 246 (tel: 209 7385). Attractively decorated music hall with sophisticated shows.

El Molino, Vila i Vila 99, Parallel (tel: 241 6383). Lots of atmosphere, noise, colour and fun in this old music hall.

El Patio Andaluz, Aribau 242 (tel: 209 3378). A choice of Andalucian specialities on the dinner menu and a good flamenco show.

La Paloma, Tigre 27. Early evening and late night sessions of dancing where extroverts like to show off. It is entertainingly 'kitsch'.

Romeria, Casanova 54. Go along here if you want to learn to dance flowing *sevillanas*.

Scala Barcelona, Passeig de Sant Joan 47 (tel: 232 6363). Dinner from an international menu followed by a big-scale international cabaret.

Jazz

Try to catch a performance by Barcelona's own Tete Montoliu and his Big Band or the Hemanos Rossy group. The 'Cave of the Dragon', **Cova del Drac**, Tuset 30, is an intimate place, long regarded as the city's top venue for jazz. Among other places to enjoy good jazz are: **L'Eixample Jazz Club**,

Diputació 341, and **Harlem**, Comtessa de Sobradiel 8. The Festival Internacional de Jazz de Barcelona is held in the Palau de la Música Catalana, Sant Francesc de Paula 2, from October to November.

Rock and Pop
Barcelona is included in most European tours by top performers and it has talented locals and expatriates. The **Palau Sant Jordi** on Montjuïc is a superb new venue for concerts and there are other venues, like the **Palau Municipal d'Esports** and **Plaça de Toros**, where big names may appear. Tickets are usually sold through record shops. Three multi-space discos which often have very good live music, including that of top international names, are: **Zeleste**, Almogàvers 122; **Studio 54**, Paral-lel 64 and **KGB**, Alegre de Dalt 55.

Cafés, Bars and Discos
New places constantly open, others close and what is in fashion loses its appeal for the trendsetters. The places selected here have shown staying power and should survive the vagaries of fashion. They offer anything from drinks before dinner (see **Food and Drink**) through to early morning disco. Some bars and discos have doormen with unfathomable criteria. The only advice is to dress 'smartly casual' and to look trendy. Some places include one drink in the entry charge. Prices can vary according to the night of the week or depending on whether there is some special event.

Before Dinner
Xampanyerias serve a good choice of cavas by the glass or bottle as well as cocktails based on cava. **El Paraigua**, Plaça Sant Miquel, behind the Ajuntament in the Ciutat Vella serves good cocktails, with stylish classical music. **Art Cava Fussina**, Fussina 6, in the avant-garde area of El Born, is also an art gallery and is popular with a young crowd. **La Cava del Palau**, Verdaguer i Callís 10, is convenient to the Palau de la Música Catalana and usually has a pianist tinkling the keys. **El Cava de Provença**, Provença 236, is a good choice in the Eixample and attracts older, middle-class regulars.

Along **Passeig del Born** are a number of cocktail bars, some with an exotic ambience and unusual drinks. On warm evenings, the bars and their terraces along the **Moll de la Fusta**, overlooking the old harbour, are an attractive

Plaça d'Espanya bathed in light

alternative. In **Boadas**, Tallers 1 (La Rambla), tiny and usually packed, the owner and her staff are expert cocktail mixers. **Café de las Artes**, València 234, is a fashionable place in the Eixample, where the drinks are reasonable. In the Sant Gervasi area, **Marcel**, Sauguès 45, and **Gimlet**, Santaló 46, are popular with a young crowd.

Cava and Coctelerías

The Catalans are very fond of their locally produced sparkling wine known as *cava* and lose no opportunity in bringing it out for family celebrations and special occasions. Barcelona is known for its *xampanyerías*, or *cava* bars, and *coctelerías* (cocktail bars). Ranging from upmarket, sophisticated, to casual and lively, they usually serve tapas and snacks. Making the rounds can be a very pleasant way of spending an evening in Barcelona.

Palau de la Música Catalana

After Dinner

Metropol, Passatge Domingo 8, a pioneer of the modern Barcelona night scene, is still one of the essential stops, especially if you like listening to black music. **Nick Havanna**, Rosselló 208, is another music bar which you should not miss, with its sensational design, hi-tech music, lighting and videos. **Zsa-Zsa**, Rosselló 156, has an elegant, calm décor with original touches, and attracts yuppies and hardworked business people in search of a revival.

Universal, Carrer de Maria Cubí, 182–4. Uptown in Sant Gervasi, this is another music hotspot with exceptional décor. **Scape**, Aribau 163, is a recent arrival on this street, which has become a focal point of the city's 'in' nightscene. It functions as a disco bar and cocktail bar in separate areas.

Satanassa, Aribau 27. A disco bar with a naughty, sexually ambivalent ambience, which often stages special nights on outrageous themes.

Centro Ciudad, Consell de Cent 294. Here you can play billiards, sit and talk, see art exhibitions and occasional live shows, listen to good music or dance.

Distrito Distinto, corner of Meridian and Aragó. A bastion of post-modernism and a haunt of the beautiful people, it is basically a disco but has live music on occasions.

Poble Espanyol

Choose well among the many places packed into this compact area and you can conveniently

have a most memorable night.
This is a suggestion for a night's
progress from around 21.00hrs:
La Cerveseria – beers from
around the world, tasty tapas.
La Cava del Poble – a good
choice of cavas.
Tablao del Carmen (tel: 325
6895) – well-rated flamenco.
Denominaciò d'Origen (tel:
325 1797) – for dinner, with
dishes and wines from Spain's
regions.
Las Torres de Avila (tel: 424
9309) – a spectacular multi-
space nocturnal venue (now a
must on the nightscene).
La Disco del Poble – to dance
away the remaining hours.

WEATHER AND WHEN TO GO

Summers are hot and humid.
The average temperature
through June to September is 74
degrees Fahrenheit (23.5
degrees Celsius) with a peak
average just over 77 degrees
Fahrenheit (25 degrees Celsius)
in July. Winters are relatively
mild with a mix of bright days
and others which are overcast
or rainy. January is usually the
coldest month, with an average
temperature around 48 degrees
Fahrenheit (9 degrees Celsius).
The most perfect weather is
usually during May and
October. Pack clothes
appropriate for the season
bearing in mind that the dress
order is to look casually smart
and comfortable. In winter and
spring take a light overcoat and
an umbrella.
The climate makes Barcelona an
all-year destination, and
whatever the season, there is a

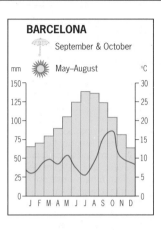

packed programme of cultural
events and entertainment.
During August, when
Barcelonans leave for the coast
or the hills, some restaurants
and other businesses may close.

HOW TO BE A LOCAL

You need to be around for a
long time and to try very hard to
become integrated as a local.
Firstly you have to decide if you
are aiming for acceptance within
the Catalan-speaking
mainstream of Barcelona
society, by the Spanish-
speaking sector or by one of the
foreign communities, among
which the French are the
strongest. In this commercially
minded city your economic
status is an important factor.
If you are wealthy your
acceptance will be faster –
immediate if you are a multi-
millionaire. But if you show real
creative talent, you can be poor
and still gain acceptance.
It is likely to block your
progress if you won't speak any

language except your own. To get in with the fastest-moving stream of Barcelona society it is essential to be conversant in Catalan. If you are really sycophantic there are ways to ingratiate yourself with every group: to Catalans say you admire their *seny* and separate culture, that you prefer Barcelona to Madrid, that people from Andalucia and Murcia are lazy; to those people and other immigrants from different parts of Spain say Catalans are tight-fisted and say how much you like whatever region they come from; to the foreigners proclaim the apparent shortcomings of Spaniards, praise their home country and say that Barcelona is the most cultured and progressive city in Spain because it has adopted so much from other countries. Certain differences between the people of Catalunya and other parts of Spain are clearly noticeable, both in temperament and looks. They tend to be more reserved and more quietly spoken than in other parts of Spain, and are often fairer of complexion. While street names, signs and many publications are in Catalan, with the language now widely spoken, you will also hear much Castilian spoken. Statistics claim that some 75 percent of Catalans are bilingual. People will generally respond in Castilian if so addressed and are, for the main part, extremely kind when asked for directions, going out of their way to be helpful. It is said that the changes in Catalunya have given the people a feeling of liberation,

which manifests itself in a new open-mindedness. As they themselves state, friendships may take time to form, but once cemented, can last a lifetime! A pleasurable pastime here is a good get together to talk or argue and *tertulias*, meetings for discussion, have long formed an important part of the scene in Barcelona. Topics may range from politics, literary themes, to the more mundane problems of housing, the rising cost of living or the eternally popular subject of sport!

If you are staying for a long time you will have to decide where you stand politically. Conservatives can choose from one of the parties which espouses Catalan nationalism or the centralist Partido Popular; for those on the left, politics range from deep red to the pale pink of the PSC, which gets the bulk of its support from immigrants to Catalunya and is affiliated to Spain's central Socialist party. Short-term visitors will probably

not involve themselves with these things, and are advised to stay out of talking about local politics. It is far better to talk about football (soccer) and show interest in 'Barça', as Barcelona Football Club is known, commiserating if the legendary club's performances have not been good. The club uniquely unites all sectors of society in expressing loyal support, and its poor fortunes on the field at times can cause a common depression. A win, especially over Real Madrid, fills the streets with ecstatic revellers. Going to see a match at Camp Nou, Europe's largest stadium, could be a priority in starting to follow local customs. You will probably not do anywhere near as well making bullfighting a subject of conversation. The ritual does not have much support in Barcelona and the weekly *corridas* during the summer attract mainly

Museu d'Art de Catalunya, Montjuïc

tourists from abroad and other parts of Spain. Participating in another weekly event, if you are a quick learner of intricate footwork, gives you a chance to immediately feel like one of the locals, even to hold hands with them. This is the *Sardana* which for many symbolises Catalan unity. Somewhat sedate, it is perhaps more satisfying to participate in than to watch. Where there is common ground among Barcelonans is the taking of leisure in the city's open spaces – its ramblas, plaças and parcs, with the new port development as a popular area for the citizens to enjoy, especially at weekends. As in all Mediterrean cities, it is outdoors that people seek their simplest pleasure, to see their neighbours and to be seen. Stroll down La Rambla any evening or go to one of the many delightful parks in the warm months, and the people of Barcelona will be on parade. Last but not least, forget about the time schedule you keep at home. Follow the local one, especially in respect of eating times and nightlife, or else you will find yourself in empty places without the atmosphere which the local people lend them. (See the **Food and Drink** and **Nightlife** sections.) Do not get irritated because many places of interest and businesses are closed during the siesta, when the locals take a long respite from the day's work. Be wise and use the time to rest from sightseeing. You will be pleased you did so if you are later discovering Barcelona by night.

La Seu towers over the Barri Gòtic

CHILDREN

It seems to be within the character of Mediterranean people to be very tolerant towards children, and Barcelona is no exception – it is hospitable to the young. The city offers a lot for them: plenty of museums and exhibitions; chances to participate in sports and other activities; entertainment and other fun. It is a city which cares about children as its adult citizens of the future, but it is not always easy for visiting children to gain access to all that is on offer. Municipal tourist offices provide information on current programmes for young people arranged by the city council. The tourist offices can also refer you to other organisations which have changing activities and special events for young people.

Theatre and Music

The **Fundació Miró** runs a programme of children's theatre (except for the four months from June to September). A weekend venue for children's theatre is the **Jove Teatre Regina**, Sèneca 22. The **Teatre Malic**, Fussina 3, also has children's theatre on Sundays from November to May. There are also neighbourhood theatre presentations, puppet shows and musical performances by and for young people in a variety of venues, indoors and in the open air, as well as clowns and other entertaining street performers.

Museums

The city's museums, such as the Museu Picasso, are often

The Sardana

Anyone may join in the *Sardana*, Catalunya's national dance, although some advance knowledge of the steps involved is preferable. The dancers join hands and form a constantly moving ring, to the strains of the local *cobla* band. Among the instruments used, two are found only in this music, the oboe-like *tenora* and *fluviol* (flute). It is usually danced on Sundays around noon in front of the Cathedral and 19.00hrs (18.30hrs in winter) in Plaça Sant Jaume, as well as throughout Catalunya, generally at weekends and on feast days.

thronged with groups of children, who are sometimes permitted to be quite noisy. This can be irritating for others wanting to take a serious interest in the exhibits. If you see a party of youngsters entering a museum or exhibition, think twice before going in yourself – it may be wise to leave your visit for another time.

Many parents will know that dragging a bored child around a museum can be an exasperating experience, but there is one museum which children are likely to enjoy very much:

Museu de la Ciència, Teodor Roviralta 55. It is extremely well planned to give an insight into various sciences and to stimulate an interest in them, especially by children (of different age groups). There are also good periodic exhibitions.

Open: Tuesday to Sunday 10.00–20.00hrs.
Closed: Monday.
Metro: Avinguda Tibidabo.

Another museum which is an option for children (of less interest to adults) is:

Museu de Cera, Passatge de la Blanca, off La Rambla (tel: 317 2649). It does not rate too highly by the standards of wax museums but has enough to be fun for children.

Open: Monday to Friday 10.00–13.30 and 16.00–19.30hrs, Saturday and Sunday 10.30–13.30 and 16.30-20.00hrs.
Metro: Drassanes, Liceu.

For children who are soccer enthusiasts there is:

Museu del FC Barcelona, Aristides Maillol s/n. In addition to various exhibits there are audiovisual presentations on the history of the club, and a view of the stadium from the presidential box.

Open: April to October, Monday to Saturday 10.00–13.00 and 15.00–18.00hrs. Holidays 10.00–14.00hrs.
Closed: Sunday.
November to March, Tuesday to Friday 10.00–13.00 and 15.00–18.00hrs; Saturday, Sunday and holidays 10.00–14.00hrs.
Closed: Monday.
Metro: Collblanc.

Rides
Bus Turìstic
This bus (number 100) operates from mid-June to mid-October and does a circuit around the city, with 15 stops at key points of interest. (See introduction to **What to See** section, page 30.) Taking the whole journey, without necessarily alighting at any of the stops, is a convenient, low-cost and untiring way of allowing children to see much of the city. The ticket also applies to use of the Tramvia Blau (tram), the Tibidabo Funicular and the Montjuïc funicular and cable car; and it allows you to claim discounts at La Muntanya Màgica, Las Golondrinas, the Zoo and Poble Espanyol.

Las Golondrinas
These are small boats which make trips in the old harbour, starting from the foot of the Columbus monument. These give a smell of sea air and a good view of the whole new

port development with its marinas, boats and quays. They leave every 30 minutes, from mid-March to mid-June and October 11.00–18.00hrs; late June 11.00–19.00hrs. July to September 11.00–20.30hrs; November to mid-March, Saturday, Sunday and public holidays only 11.00–18.00hrs. *Metro*: Drassanes.

Cable Cars

Since 1929 taking a cable car ride high across the harbour has been a favourite outing for children. The towers look a bit ancient, but do not be put off. The service runs between Barceloneta and the Miramar point on Montjuïc, with an intermediate tower (an optional stop or alighting point) on Barcelona Moll (quay). The hours of operation are rather variable so it is wise to enquire from a tourist office when you are in the city.

If you want to combine a funicular ride with a cable car trip, take the funicular from the lower base near the Paral-lel metro station, and then a cable car across the Parc d'Atraccions de Montjuïc castle, where the military museum may be of interest to some children.

Amusement Parks

The **Parc d'Atraccions de Montjuïc** is a family fun park but perhaps more appealing to adults. There are some 40 machines of various sorts, and a small open-air theatre where entertainments are offered in summer. From late June to early September it is open every day except Mondays. During the rest of the year it is open on weekends and holidays only, but check exact hours with a tourist office.

La Muntanya Màgica is the amusement park on Tibidabo, the high point of the Collserola range of hills. It has recently been renovated and is a well-run place for all the family. Getting there is something children will enjoy too. Take the metro to Avinguda Tibidabo station and then the old (but not rickety) Tramvia Blau (tram) to the lower station of a funicular which creaks gently up to the summit. Times of services relate to the opening hours of the amusement park, so check locally. There are different types of tickets depending on what you want to do in the amusement park, how much time you want to spend there, your age and the like, so be sure that you get the ticket that suits you. The most essential experience is to take a ride on the Avion Tibiar – it gives a whirring thrill to any child (and great views of Barcelona). The Museu d'Automatas with its human and animal robots, games and models will also delight some children.

A **zoo** is not really an amusement park but Barcelona's caters well for children. Besides its star attraction of Floc de Neu (Snowflake), the albino gorilla, and other animals, there are performances by dolphins and parrots. It also has a section where children can touch farm animals and pets. (See also **What to See**, page 65).

The garden of fantasies, **Parc Güell**, is also very popular with children. (See separate entry, page 56.)

Poble Espanyol

For children this can be a fascinating place to visit and see the variety of architecture from all over Spain. There are also periodic entertainments for them, presented in the main square. (See also **What to See**, pages 61–2).

Port Aventura

This spectacular new theme park, opened in May 1995, is now 'the place' to take the children for a day trip or longer. Located south of Barcelona, between Salou and Vila-seca (Costa Daurada), it is less than two hours away by car, rail or organised tour. The park offers numerous activities in exotic Mexican, Chinese, Polynesian and Mediterranean settings.

Activities

A very gentle activity is rowing a boat on the small lake in the Parc de la Ciutadella throughout the year, or during the winter in Parc de la Creueta del Coll. From June to September the lake of Parc de la Creueta del Coll becomes a favourite swimming place for children. Then there are the beaches – a big choice north and south of the city. One of the better ones near the city centre is Mar-bella in the Poble Nou district. Children enjoy the cycling and scenery on Montjuïc, but they should exercise care as the area is used by motoring schools to put pupils through their paces. Bicitram, Avinguda Marqués de l'Argentera 15 (tel: 792 2841) rents cycles.

TIGHT BUDGET

Investigate what budget holiday packages to Barcelona are available from your country: these often work out far cheaper than arranging travel and accommodation yourself. If you are looking for low-cost

Screaming fun, La Muntanya Màgica

TIGHT BUDGET

accommodation on the spot, the best area for budget pensions is within the Ciutat Vella, but avoid the part on the seaward side of Carrer Ferran and Carrer de l'Hospital. The district of Gràcia also has budget accommodation and is conveniently situated for exploring the city without too much expenditure on transport. There are budget pensions in the Eixample, best in the area of Sants station and the Sagrada Família. You can stay cheaply in other parts of the city but there will be more trudging around finding a place you like and inspecting the rooms on offer. Camping is another possible alternative (see **Directory** pages 114–15).

You will find the biggest concentration of budget eating places in the Ciutat Vella. Look along Carrers dels Tallers, Sitges, Santa Anna and Comtal, on either side of the top end of La Rambla.

Spain in a nutshell at Poble Espanyol

- All over the city there are unassuming bars or *sesones* with low cost food and drink. Gràcia is a good area to look.
- Avoid places which display an array of credit card signs.
- Ordering a choice of *tapas* or *raciones* (larger portions) can work out more costly than taking the *menú del día*.
- Beer is cheaper if you ask for *una caña* (draught), and a *vino de la case* (house wine) will be the lowest priced.
- Buy food and drink in a market or shop to make up a meal which you can enjoy outdoors in one of the city's many delightful open spaces.
- A small supply of food and drink in your room is a saving standby, but avoid turning your room into a kitchen.
- Walking is not only the cheapest way of getting around the city, it is also the best way to get to know it. Cost saving options for public transport are mentioned in the **Directory** (pages 120–1).

- For entertainment, taking an evening *passeig* (stroll) and indulging in people-watching is the cheapest option.
- If you want to sit at a fashionable open-air café, make the most of the cost by lingering over your drink (the locals do).
- Instead of La Rambla, go to the less expensive Avinguda de Mistral, south of Plaça d'Espanya. It has a lively atmosphere in warm weather, with open-air bars and a younger crowd.
- For details of free entertainment, consult the local press, look at billboards, enquire at tourist offices and ask the Cultural Information Centre at La Rambla 99.
- For budget shopping, avoid the high class districts. Go into the other residential areas such as Gràcia, and visit the markets.

SPECIAL EVENTS

As well as the events below, each of the city's barris has its own annual celebrations in honour of its patron saint.

January
On the 6th the Three Kings, **Reis Mags**, arrive by boat. Seated on grand floats they progress through the city, showering the crowds with sweets.

February/March
Carnival closes on Ash Wednesday with the symbolic burial of a sardine. Preceding days are merry, colourful and hectic. Celebrations in the nearby seaside town of Sitges are the most spectacular and uninhibited.

April
Sant Jordi (St George), Catalunya's patron saint, has his day on the 23rd. It is also the day when couples express their love by gifts of a book to the man and a rose to the woman. On and just before **El Dia de la Palma** (Palm Sunday) huge markets sell decorative palms. **Festival of Old Music** (through May).
The Fundació Miró and Nick Havanna are main venues for the **Festival of Contemporary Music** (through May and June). Sitges hosts an **International Theatre Festival** towards the end of the month.

May
Stalls selling herbs, honey and crystallised fruits are set up in Carrer de l'Hospital (off La Rambla) for the **Fira de Sant Ponç**, whose day is on the 11th. **Maig Coral**, a season of choir music, through June.

June
The **summer solstice** is celebrated with bonfires, fireworks and an abundance of merrymaking.
Sant Joan's day on the 24th, a public holiday, gives time to recover.
The **Grec Festival** starts this month and runs through to early August, with music, dance and theatre, which is of a high standard and noted internationally.
Barcelona's **International Film Festival** starts towards the end of the month and runs for two weeks.
Flamenco Festival during the last two weeks.

SPECIAL EVENTS

Greek Theatre

Each year, with variable dates between June and July, sees the staging of the Barcelona Summer Festival. Known as the 'Grec', performances of theatre, dance and music are held in various venues, which include the 'Teatro Grec' in Montjuïc, Poble Espanyol, Plaça del Rei, Palua de la Música Catalana and Parc Güell.

September

Diada de Catalunya, the Catalan national day on the 11th, marks not a victory but the taking of the city by Felipe V in 1714. Political manifestations are the order of the day.

Setmana Gran is the week leading up to the 24th – the day of La Mercè, the city's patron saint, who is favoured with its principal fiesta. A special programme of theatre and

Museu Maricel, Sitges

concerts is arranged. Parades feature *gegants* (giants) and *caps grossos* (big heads); *castellers* build their human towers in Plaça Sant Jaume; the *Sardana*, Catalunya's staid national dance, is danced to the strains of the *cobla* band wherever there is space; and the wine and cava flow freely.

October to November

International Jazz Festival held at the Palau de la Música Catalana.

November

International Festival of Fantastic Cinema in Sitges, 26 miles (42km) south of Barcelona.

December

The **Fira Santa Llucia** starts on the 13th, the saint's feast day, when the plaça in front of the Cathedral and the alleys around it are filled with bright stalls selling Christmas gifts (including many craft items), decorations and model nativity scenes.

Dancing Giants and Dragons

Giant figures play an important part in traditional Catalan folklore and feature in many musical and theatrical programmes which take place in various outdoor areas, in front of the Cathedral, Plaça Sant Jaume, Plaça del Rei and Sot de Migdia, to name a few. Most colourful are the 'Ball de Gegants' (Dance of the Giants) and the 'Correfoc' when dragons, demons and other such creatures prance about the Ciutat Vella scattering firecrackers.

SPORT

In its sports amenities and the quality of its venues Barcelona now rates among the best-provided cities in the world. The main spectator sports are soccer, basketball, athletics, cycling, swimming and tennis. To find out what is on during your stay, look in newspapers or the specialist daily, *El Mundo Deportivo*. Information is also available from the Sports Division of the Ajuntament, Avinguda del Estadi s/n (tel: 325 4362). Exhibitions on sporting themes are held in the Museu i Centre d'Estudis de l'Esport 'Dr Melcior Colet', Buenos Aires 56–8.

What follows is a selection of places for participant sports which are open to the public:

Sports Complex

Can Caralleu, Esports s/n (tel: 204 6905). A pleasant, well-run complex with covered and uncovered swimming pools, and courts for tennis, volleyball and *fronton* (or *pelota* – a fast-moving ball game of northern Spain). Classes are available. *Open*: 08.00–23.00hrs for tennis, but it is advisable to check opening times and availability of the various facilities.

Bowling

Bowling Center AMF, Sabino de Arana 6 (tel: 330 5048). *Open*: Monday to Saturday 11.00–02.00hrs, Sunday 11.00hrs–midnight.
Pedralbes Bowling Alley, Bolera Pedralbes, Avinguda del Doctor Marañón 11 (tel: 333 0352). Offers classes.

Open: 10.00–02.00hrs. (Friday and Saturday 10.00–04.00hrs).

Cycling

Over weekends and on holidays, from 10.00hrs to the early evening, **Bicitram** hire out a choice of bicycles from three depots: Avinguda Marqués d'Argentera 15 (for rides in the Parc de la Ciutadella and seaside area); Carretera Aigües s/n (convenient for exploring the area of the Collserola hills); Aragó 19 (for inner city rides). **Bicisport** offer a similar service (convenient for cycling around Montjuïc) from their depot near the Palau Nacional.

Equestrian

El Ecuestre Escola Municipal d'Hípica La Fuxarda, Avinguda Muntanyans 1 (tel: 426 1066). Centre providing riding lessons giving special attention to children of school age.

Golf

It is necessary to present your membership card of a nationally federated club before you can play. These are the three clubs near Barcelona, listed in order of green fee costs, starting with the highest (and poshest). An indication is given of distance from the city. All have comprehensive facilities including swimming pools. It is advisable to make advance enquiries and bookings by mail or telephone.
El Prat Golf Club, Apartado de Correus 10 (08820), El Prat de Llobregat (tel: 379 0278). Nine miles (15km). Three courses and a venue for international competitions.

SPORT

Sant Cugat Golf Course, (08190) Sant Cugat del Vallès (tel: 674 3958). 12½ miles (20km).

Vallromanes Golf Club, Apartado de Correus 43 (08170) Montornès del Vallès (tel: 568 0362). 14 miles (23km). You can, however, play golf at the following without a licence: **Golf Range Diagonal**, Plaça Mireia, s/n (tel: 473 9671); **La Cancha**, Calvet 67–69 (tel: 209 2589); **Escuela Nevada Golf**, Passeig Sant Gervasi 81 (tel: 418 7434); **Only Golf-Londres Swing**, Londres 41 (tel: 405 0605).

Skating

FC Barcelona, Avinguda Aristides Maillol s/n (tel: 350 9411). A division of the Barcelona Football Club. Classes in skating and ice hockey are available. Enquire locally about opening times and other details.

Inside the Olympic stadium at Montjuïc

Squash

Squash Barcelona, Avinguda del Doctor Marañón 17 (tel: 334 0258). It has 14 squash courts and two for racket ball. Coaching is available. Telephone to reserve a court. *Open*: 08.00hrs–midnight. (Saturday and Sunday 10.00–22.00hrs).

Swimming

There are beaches north and south of the city, and a number of pools are open to the public, for example **Club Natació de Catalunya**, Carrer Ramiro de Maeztu s/n (tel: 213 4344). Indoor and outdoor pools. Classes. *Open*: 07.00–14.00hrs.

Tennis

Vall Parc Club, Carretera de la Arrabassada 97 (tel: 212 6789). Has 14 tennis courts, a pelota court and three squash courts. Prices are higher at night. Telephone to book a court. *Open*: 08.00–midnight. (See also **Can Caralleu**, page 111, where court hire costs are lower.)

DIRECTORY

Contents

Arriving

Entry Formalities

You require a valid passport to enter Spain. Nationals of European Union countries, USA and Japan, do not need a visa for stays of up to 90 days. Check the current situation with a Spanish tourist office or Spanish consulate in your own country. Visitors from most countries require no medical documents.

By Air

Iberia, Spain's national airline, and the airlines of other countries operate direct connections between Barcelona and most European capitals. Charter companies operate connections with a number of European airports, especially in the summer. There are also direct connections with New York, Tokyo and Rio de Janeiro, and more inter-continental services are expected. Other inter-continental flights have to be made through Madrid. Connections with Spanish cities are by Iberia or Aviaco, its affiliate. Between 06.30 and 22.30hrs Iberia operates a regular shuttle, Puente Aereo, between Barcelona and Madrid, on weekdays every 15 minutes between 06.30 and 08.45hrs and every half hour from 09.00 to 22.30hrs. El Prat airport is 7½ miles (12km) south of the city on the C244 autovia. It has four terminals and offers comprehensive services. Money exchange facilities are available 07.30–22.45hrs daily. The tourist office is open Monday to Saturday 09.30–20.30hrs, Sunday and holidays 09.30–15.00hrs. There is a hotel reservations desk. Porters charge by the number of bags. A train service connects with Sants and Plaça Catalunya stations every 30 minutes between 06.30 and 23.00hrs, with a journey time of 18 minutes and 24 minutes respectively. The Airbus operates between the airport and Plaça Catalunya every 15 minutes Monday to Friday and every 30 minutes Saturday, Sunday and holidays.

DIRECTORY

By Bus
Regular bus services from a number of countries connect with the Spanish operators Iberbus, Vía Eurolines and Julià. Barcelona Nord Coach Station (Estació d'Autobusos Barcelona Nord) has good amenities. Nearest metro station is Glòries.

By Car
Barcelona is 92 miles (150km) south of La Jonquera, the frontier point with France, on autopista A7/A17 (E4). Motorway access from the rest of Spain is along autopista A2/A7 (E4). There can be lengthy tailbacks into the city at daily peak times from around 08.00 to 11.00hrs and 18.30 to 21.00hrs, and horrific ones in the late afternoon during summer on Sundays and public holidays.

By Rail
Long distance and international trains now operate from

Beaches are in easy reach

Barcelona-Estació de França, Avinguda Marqués de l'Argentera s/n. Rail information: National (tel: 490 0202); International (tel: 490 1122). Information and ticket sales: open daily 06.30–22.30hrs. Money exchange (*caixa*) open daily 08.00–11.00 and 15.00–22.00hrs. Closed 25 and 26 December and 1 and 6 January. Left-luggage lockers open 06.00–23.00hrs. Estació de Sants, Plaça Paisos Catalans s/n (Plaça Espanya) operates domestic services, including trains to the French border in Cerbère and La Tour de Carol. Information: (tel: 490 1122). Money exchange: open daily 08.00–22.00hrs. Closed as Estació de França. Left-luggage lockers open 04.30–00.30hrs. Porters charge by the number of bags. Many services from here also stop at Plaça Catalunya and Passeig de Gràcia.

By Sea
Trasmediterránea run regular passenger and car ferry connections with the Balearic Islands and there is a weekly connection with Livorno (Italy) by Alimar. Barcelona is also a port of call for cruise liners.

Camping
Within about ten miles (16km) of Barcelona there are 12 camp sites with a capacity of over 10,000 places. They are mostly to the south, off the C246 road past the airport towards Castelldefels. Information is available from Spanish tourist offices overseas. The Generalitat publishes a *Catalunya Camping* brochure annually. The Barcelona

Camping Association (Associació de Càmpings de Barcelona) is at Gran Via CC 608, 3° (tel: 412 5955).

Consulates

Many countries already represented in Barcelona are strengthening their consular presence and other countries are opening new consulates. Latest listings from tourist offices and the police.
Canada: Via Augusta 125 (tel: 209 0634).
Republic of Ireland: Gran Via Carles III 94 (tel: 491 5021).
United Kingdom: Avinguda Diagonal 477 (tel: 419 9044).
United States of America: Passeig Reina Elisenda 23 (tel: 280 2227).

Crime

Handbag and camera snatching, pocket-picking, running off with unattended luggage or bags and breaking into cars are the principal crimes against visitors. Muggings for jewellery and cash may happen in the seedier areas. At night, especially at weekends and in outlying districts, bands of hooligans sometimes threaten and rob passengers on metro trains and buses. The last part of metro line 1 and bus number 605 are the most notorious. The following precautions are advisable: deposit valuables (travellers' cheques, cash, passports, etc) in a hotel safety deposit box; wear handbags and cameras across your chest and wallets in front trouser pockets; do not flaunt jewellery or cash; keep an eye on your parcels and luggage; do not leave valuables in a car (or

anything in sight that might tempt a thief); avoid lonely, seedy and dark areas, use taxis late at night. However, crime is no worse than in most cities.

Chemist see Pharmacies

Customs Regulations

Items for personal use may be imported from one EU country to another without payment of duty. For cigarettes, cigars, wines, spirits and perfumes, maximum limits have been established, with customs leviable on amounts exceeding them and only small amounts may be purchased as duty-free goods. For information on current allowances and regulations consult your tour operator or the Spanish Consulate in your country.

Disabled People

Barcelona shows awareness of the needs of disabled people in its provision of special amenities such as ramps, wider doorways and toilets. Special needs should be stated and full enquiries made before making final reservations. Spain's private organisation for disabled people is ECOM, Balmes 311, 08006 Barcelona (tel: 217 3882).

Driving

Breakdown

Detroit, Biscaia 326 (tel: 351 1203) provide a 24-hour towing-in (*grúas*) service and have a workshop. An insurance policy bought from your motoring organisation may provide special arrangements. In the case of rental vehicles, contact the rental company. These

organisations have reciprocal arrangements with organisations overseas, and can advise non-members in case of need: Reial Automòbil Club de Catalunya, Santaló 8 (tel: 200 3311; for 24-hour service tel: 200 0755.
Caravan Club Barcelona, Aragó 416 (tel: 245 0500).

Car Rental
Below is a selection of firms with their city office addresses and telephone numbers:
Atesa, Balmes 141 (tel: 237 8140)
Avis, Casanovas 209 (tel: 209 9533)
Europcar, Consell de Cent 363 (tel: 488 2398)
Hertz, Tuset 10 (tel: 217 3248)
Ital-Budget, Travessera Gràcia 71 (tel: 201 2199)
Julià Rent-a-Car, Santa Eulàlia 176–180 (tel: 431 1100)
Tot Car, Avinguda Josep Tarradellas 93 (tel: 410 1349)
Vanguard, Londres 31 (tel: 439 3880). Also rent motorcycles.
For rental of caravans:
Caravanas Marte, Santa Ana 28 (tel: 317 6234).
Other vehicles for hire:
Auto-Antic, Paco Mutlió (tel: 723 8101).

Documents
Licences issued by European Union countries are acceptable. People from other countries should have an international driving licence. Spain's Ministry of Transport publishes a leaflet of advice for drivers (available from frontier posts or tourist offices). If driving to Spain, take advice and get information from a motoring organisation in your country before setting off, and

buy appropriate insurance. Third party insurance is compulsory in Spain. Travellers are advised to obtain a Green Card (which includes a bail bond in case of accident) from their own insurance company. Road signs and rules are generally in line with those of other European countries (with some eccentricities).

Driving in Barcelona
Barcelonans have a driving 'discipline' which bemuses most visitors and terrifies nervous drivers (and pedestrians). Your time in the city may be more relaxing if you do not use a car.

Fuel
The fuel sold is normal (92 octane); super (96 octane); gas-oil (diesel); and *sin plomo* (lead-free). Butane gas for cars is available (24 hours) from Gas-Auto, Carrer K, Zona Franca.

Parking
Street parking is limited. Spaces are indicated by blue road and kerb markings, and tickets are bought from machines on the pavement. Inner city car parks are inexpensive by international standards and are the best places to leave your car.

Electricity
The supply is 220 or 225 volts AC and 110 or 125 in some bathrooms and older buildings. Plugs have two round pins.

Emergency Telephone Numbers
Police help for visitors: 301 9060. This is a 24-hour service with interpreters for English-,

French- and German-speakers. The office is at La Rambla 43 (opposite the lane into Plaça Reial).

Emergency Medical and Ambulance Service: 061
Ambulances: 329 7766 or 329 9701 (Municipal) and 300 2020 (Creu Roja)
Doctors: 212 8585 or 255 5555
Traffic accidents: 092
National Police: 091
Municipal Police: 092
Fire Brigade: 080

Entertainment Information
Daily newspapers (see **Media**, page 118), the weekly *Guia del Ocio* and the monthly *Vivir en Barcelona* have comprehensive listings. Look at billboards and pick up leaflets and information from tourist offices and from the Palau Virreina, La Rambla 99. The municipal information service (tel: 010) is a good source of information in Castilian, Catalan, English and French.

Entry Formalities see **Arriving**

Health
Residents of European Union countries are entitled to reciprocal treatment from the Spanish health service if they hold form E110, E111 or E112, obtainable from post offices. But the best advice for all foreign visitors to Spain is to buy a travel insurance policy from a reputable company which provides comprehensive cover in case of accident and illness. It is also wise to carry a photocopy of prescriptions for any medication you are taking. Problems are most likely to arise from over-indulgence in

Look out for details in La Rambla

drink and food by people in a holiday mood and caught up in Barcelona's heady nightlife. In summer, health problems may be caused by too much sun and eating mayonnaise or 'sad' salads and tapas; or they may be a reaction to unfamiliar tap water (so stick to bottled water).

Hospitals
There are a number of private hospitals and dental clinics, and three centrally located public hospitals with departments for *urgencias* (emergencies):
Nearest the Ciutat Vella: Hospital Sant Pau, Carrer Sant Antoni Maria Claret 167 (tel: 347 3133).
In Esquerra de l'Eixample: Hospital Clínic, Casanovas 143 (tel: 323 1414).
Near the Sagrada Família: Hospital Creu Roja, Dos de Maig 301 (tel: 235 9300).

DIRECTORY

Holidays

Barris have their separate feast days when places close. Besides the variable dates of Easter and Whitsun, the principal holidays are:
New Year's Day (1 January)
Reis Mags (6 January)
Sant Josep (19 March)
Sant Joan (24 June)
Assumpció (15 August)
La Mercè (24 September)
Hispanitat (12 October)
Tot Sants (1 November)
Dia de la Constitució
(6 December)
Immaculada Concepció
(8 December)
Nadal (25 December)
Sant Esteve (26 December)

Lost Property

Go to the Lost Property Office:
Servei De Troballers,
Ajuntament, Plaça de Sant Jaume
(tel: 402 7000). *Open:* weekdays
09.30–13.30hrs. Advise your
consulate about loss of personal

Plaça Reial - beautiful but shady

documents and if necessary contact credit card companies (see **Money Matters**, page 119).

Media

Newspapers

Many daily newspapers from other European countries are available by the afternoon. International editions are on sale in the morning. *El Pais*, Spain's most respected national daily, publishes a Barcelona edition and, on Fridays, a good 'what's on' guide. *La Vanguardia* is the oldest of Barcelona's dailies; the newer, popular *El Periodico* concentrates on local news. The two dailies published in Catalan are *Avui* and *Diari de Barcelona*.

Magazines

Spain publishes a huge number of magazines, the weekly *Cambio 16* is a respected news magazine in the *Times/Newsweek* format. For

sensationalism and scandal *Hola* is the leader.

Television

There are six television channels of which two are in Catalan – TV3 and Barcelona TV (also Castilian). TV1 and TV2 and others are mostly in Castilian. Canal + is a paying channel in addition.

Radio

Among the many stations *Cadena SER* on MW 828 kHz is the most popular, with easy-listening music and local news.

Money Matters

Banks

Barcelona abounds with banks, local and foreign. Savings banks, mostly also offering exchange facilities, are called *caixas* in Catalan. *Open:* Monday to Thursday 08.30–16.30hrs, Friday 08.30–14.00hrs, Saturday (main branches only) 08.30–13.00hrs. June to September, Monday to Friday 08.30–14.00hrs, Saturdays closed. Money exchange facilities are available outside these hours at the airport, Sants railway station and the Caixa de Pensions, La Rambla 30. Cashpoints issuing money around the clock with use of a credit card and PIN are plentiful.

Credit Cards

The major credit, charge and direct debit cards are widely accepted, including American Express (tel: 217 0070); Diners Club (tel: 302 1428); MasterCard and Visa (tel: 315 2512).

Currency

The peseta is available in these denominations – notes: 10,000, 5,000, 2,000, 1,000; coins: 500, 200, 100, 50, 25, 10, 5.

Tax

IVA, a value-added tax, is currently applied at six per cent on most goods and services and at 12 or 33 per cent on luxury items and some services. People resident outside the EU can gain exemption from tax on large individual purchases. Shops will provide information.

Opening Times

See **Shopping, Money Matters, Post Office** and **Public Transport**. Businesses work from Monday to Friday, but have varying hours depending on their location, type and the season. In the summer many businesses work *horas intensivas*, 08.00–15.00hrs. For the rest of the year, general hours are 09.00–14.00 and 16.00–20.00hrs. Official organisations are generally open to the public from Monday to Friday 08.00–15.00hrs.

Pharmacies

These are known as *farmacias*. As well as selling prescription medicines they will provide free advice about minor injuries or ailments and suggest a non-prescription treatment from their stocks. They are easily identified by a big green cross sign and follow normal shopping hours. During other times they will display a sign indicating the nearest *farmacia de guardia*, which will be open. Local papers also list these.

DIRECTORY

Places of Worship

Most churches are Catholic. Catholic masses are also said in English, French, German and Italian. Other denominations and faiths with communities in the city include: Anglican, Evangelical, Greek Orthodox, Jehovah's Witness, Jewish, Mormon, Muslim and Seventh Day Adventist. Tourist offices and consulates have information on places and times of worship.

Police

Officers of the three police organisations all wear blue uniforms and have different, sometimes confusingly overlapping roles.

Guardia Urbana: The municipal police are mainly responsible for traffic, and have blue and white checked bands on their vehicles and caps.

Sagrada Família

Policia Nacional: Spain's national police are responsible for law and order and internal security. It is to them that you should report a crime or loss and make a *denuncia* (statement). Their main office at Via Laietana 49 (tel: 302 6325) provides interpreter services. There is also a mobile office at the Plaça de Catalunya end of La Rambla or half way down it.

Mossos d'Esquadra: Catalunya's police force operates mostly in country areas. Officers protect the Generalitat building.

Post Office

The main post office (*correus*) is at Plaça Antonio López. *Open*: Monday to Friday 09.00–21.00hrs, Saturday 09.00–14.00hrs. Other offices: Monday to Saturday 09.00–14.00hrs. Mail can be sent to you at: Lista de Correus, Plaça Antonio López, 08000 BARCELONA, Catalunya, Spain. Take personal identification when collecting. Post boxes are yellow and some have different sections for different destinations.

Public Transport

On arrival collect the latest *Guia del Transporte Público de Barcelona y su Area Metropolitana* issued by the TMB (Metropolitan Transport Corporation). They have offices at Sants station; Plaça de Catalunya; the Universitat metro station; Ronda Sant Pau 43; and Avinguda Borbó 12. *Open*: 08.00–19.00hrs. From these offices you can get current information about, and buy, *targetes multiviage i abonaments* (multi-journey and saver tickets). These are also available from metro stations, some buses and *caixas* (savings banks). A telephone information service operates (tel: 336 0000).

Air

Many foreign airlines have offices in the city. The main offices of Iberia are at Passeig de Gràcia 30 and Diputació 258. For information – Infoiberia (tel: 412 5667); domestic bookings (tel: 412 7020); international bookings (tel: 412 4748).

Bus

There is a comprehensive bus network. For general information on public transport (tel: 412 0000). A *tarjeta metropolitana* is sold at an *estanco* or *tabac* and is a 10-ticket carnet valid on buses and the metro. This is a most economical and efficient way of getting around. Otherwise, one-price tickets are bought from the driver. Most buses operate from around 05.30–22.30hrs, plus a few night services.

Metro

Four underground lines, I, III, IV and V, interconnect with the under- and overground train service run by the Generalitat, which extends beyond the city. Maps of the network are displayed at all stations. For metro journeys there is a single fare regardless of distance. *Open*: Monday to Thursday 05.00–23.00hrs; Friday, Saturday and evenings before public holidays 05.00–01.00hrs; Sunday 06.00–midnight; mid-week holidays 06.00–23.00hrs.

Taxis

Black and yellow taxis show a green light when available for hire and can be flagged down in the street. Standard rates are shown on the meter and there are supplements for baggage or for trips departing from railway stations and the airport. For information about the 'taxi card' (a credit card), telephone 412 2000. Telephone numbers of some taxi operators: 357 7755; 358 1111; 490 2222. For chauffeur-driven cars: Limousine Service, Montjamar 24 (tel: 429 1388) is one of several companies.

Trains

RENFE is Spain's national railway company. It also operates *rodalies* (suburban trains). Full information can be obtained from travel agents, from RENFE stations (the one at Plaça de Catalunya is central) or by telephoning 490 0202.

Senior Citizens

Ask travel agents about special package holidays in Barcelona for senior citizens from your country. Within the city there are good amenities and many special events for senior citizens, but access for visitors may be limited and fluency in Catalan or Castilian is usually needed to appreciate them fully.

Student and Youth Travel

Barcelona is a good city in which to be young. Regional and municipal authorities, other organisations and young people themselves provide many amenities and there is always a full programme of special

BARCELONA metro & suburban lines

events. There are seven youth hostels and some 30 'youth houses' (run by young people), as well as cheap bed and breakfast places. Some useful addresses are:
CIAJ, Ferran 32 (tel: 402 7800). *Metro*: Liceu. A youth information and advice centre – the best source of advice for young people.
Direcció General de Joventut Generalitat de Catalunya, Calàbria 147 (tel: 483 8383). *Metro*: Rocafort or Entença. Contact for youth cards, which provide discounts at many different places.

V.MMC V2293 UDN.1

user no. 9C02117

Telephones

Many hotels provide telephone, telefax and telegram services, but add sizeable supplements. The code for Barcelona (city and province) is 93 and is used for calls from other provinces. To call a Barcelona number from outside Spain dial the international service code applicable in your country, then 34 (Spain), 3 (Barcelona) and the seven-digit number. Public phone booths are plentiful. They take 500, 200, 100, 50, 25, 10 and 5 peseta coins and some accept credit cards. Instructions for use are displayed in a number of languages, as are provincial and international dialling codes. Many bars also have telephones for use by customers. To make direct international calls put at least 200 pesetas in the groove at the top (or in the slot of some telephones), dial 07 and wait for a changed tone, then dial the country code, town code (without the initial 0) and number. At the Telefonica *locutorio*, Fontanella 4 (Plaça de Catalunya) you can get assistance, and make reversed-charge calls. You pay after your call. You can also do this at El Corte Inglés (see page 88). A cheap rate applies from 22.00 to 08.00hrs. For telephone information, dial 003.

Telefax, telex and telegram services are available at the Correus, Plaça Antoni López, (08.00–22.00hrs) and at Ronda Universitat 23, (09.00–19.00hrs). Many businesses also offer telefax services. For telegrams by telephone (24-hour service), telephone 322 2000.

Time
Barcelona is two hours ahead of GMT (Greenwich Mean Time) in the summer and one hour ahead in the winter.

Tipping
Most hotel and restaurant bills include a service charge, but you may still want to give a tip of between 5 and 10 per cent in restaurants and for special services in hotels. At bars leave less than 5 per cent from your change. The same applies to taxis. Other people who expect tips are car park attendants, doormen, hairdressers,

shoeshines, lavatory attendants and tour guides.

Toilets
Public lavatories are few and far between, but there is an increasing number of lavatory cabins. There are toilet facilities at department stores and most museums and cultural centres. Bars and restaurants have facilities for their customers.

Tourist Offices

Overseas
Turespaña, part of Spain's Ministry of Tourism operates offices in several countries. Addresses are liable to change, so ask locally.

Australia: 203 Castlereagh Street, Suite 21, Level 2, Sydney NSW 2000.

Canada: 102 Bloor Street West, 14th Floor, Toronto.

UK: 57–8, St James Street, London SW1A 1LD.

USA: 665 Fifth Avenue, New York 10022; 8383 Wilshire Boulevard, Suite 960, Beverly Hills, California 90211.

In Barcelona
See also **Arriving**, page 113. The Generalitat has an office at Gran Via de les Corts Catalanes 658 (tel: 301 7443). *Open*: Monday to Friday 09.00–19.00hrs, Saturday 09.00–14.00hrs. From late June to the end of September the Ajuntament operates offices in Plaça Sant Jaume and the Palau de la Virreina, La Rambla 99. *Open*: Monday to Saturday 08.00–14.00hrs. In the summer there are also helpful, red-coated guides, who wander La Rambla to assist visitors.

LANGUAGE

There are two official languages in Catalonia: Catalan, the language of the region, and Castilian (Spanish), the official language of Spain. This short list of Catalan words and phrases will help you to show courtesy, understand signs, ask directions, shop and order services. The person may speak your language, so ask.

do you speak Castilian/English/ French/German? ¿parleu castellà/ anglès/francès/alecany?

yes/no si/no

please speak a little slower si us plau, parleu una mica més a poc a poc

good morning bon dia

good afternoon bona tarda

good evening bona nit

goodbye adéu-siau

please si us plau

thank you gràcies

my name is...em dic...

what is your name? ¿com us dieu?

where is...? ¿On és...?

is it far/nearby? ¿és lluny/a prop?

left/right/ahead esquerra/dret/tot seguit

avenue/boulevard/passage avinguda/passeig/passatge

street/square carrer/plaça

church/monastery/palace/school esglesia/monestir/palau/escola

open/closed oberta/tancat

hour/day/week/month/year hora/dia (jorn)/setmana/mes/any

Monday to Sunday dilluns, dimarts, dimecres, dijous, divendres, dissabte, diumenge

yesterday/today/tomorrow ahir/avui/demà

I would like... voldria...

how much? ¿quant val?

do you have a larger/smaller/cheaper one/another colour? ¿en té de més gran/més petit/més bon preu/un altre color?

Numbers	
one	un
two	dos
three	tres
four	quatre
five	cinc
six	sis
seven	set
eight	vuit
nine	nou
ten	deu

Local produce displayed with flair

INDEX

Page numbers in *italics* refer to illustrations.

Acknowledgements
The Automobile Association wishes to thank the following photographers and libraries for their assistance in the preparation of this book.
PETER WILSON took all the photographs not listed below (© AA PHOTO LIBRARY).
AA PHOTO LIBRARY 25 Olympic Stadium and 87 El Corte Galerias (P Enticknap), 114 Camping.
MARY EVANS PICTURE LIBRARY 16 19th-century Barcelona, 20 Civil War.
NATURE PHOTOGRAPHERS LTD 75 Cistus, 76 Rock Bunting (K J Carlson), 77 Zaragoza (P R Sterry), 78 Ordesa National Park (R O Bush).
SPECTRUM COLOUR LIBRARY 31 Olympic Stadium, 73 Cliffs north of Tossa.

Contributors for this revision:
Researcher/verifier: Mona King

Thanks also to the **Spanish Tourist Office, London**; **Turisme de Barcelona, Barcelona**; and **Iberia International Airlines of Spain** for their assistance with this revision.

Copy editor for original edition: Antonia Hebbert